Candleholders
in America

1650 - 1900

Also by
Joseph T. Butler

———◆———

American Antiques, 1800-1900:
A Collector's History and Guide

Four brass candlesticks, probably English, c. 1825-1830, used in the dining room at Cortlandt Manor at Croton-on-Hudson, New York. These candlesticks have always remained in the Manor House and are part of the Van Cortlandt family collection. *Sleepy Hollow Restorations*

Candleholders in America
1650 - 1900

A Comprehensive Collection of
American and European Candle Fixtures
Used in America

"Elizabeth Bálya Somody"

Joseph T. Butler "1970"

Bonanza Books · New York

© MCMLXVII, by Joseph T. Butler

Library of Congress Catalog Card Number: 67-15986

Printed in the United States of America

Designed by Mary Ciani

This edition published by Bonanza Books,
a division of Crown Publishers, Inc.

a   b   c   d   e   f   g   h

Acknowledgments

MANY INDIVIDUALS HAVE KINDLY ASSISTED IN THE PREPARATION of this book. Credit for ownership of the objects reproduced is given with each of the photographs. However, I should like to thank sincerely the private collectors who have so graciously provided me with photographs of objects from their collections, objects that for the most part are not often seen publicly. They are: Mrs. Edsel B. Ford, Grosse Point, Michigan; Miss Helen C. Frick, New York City; Colonel and Mrs. Edgar W. Garbisch, New York City; Mr. and Mrs. Bertram K. Little, Brookline, Massachusetts; Mr. and Mrs. Samuel Schwartz, Paterson, New Jersey; Mrs. Giles Whiting, New York City; and Louis B. Young, Cumberland, Maryland.

Others have been especially helpful by providing information and photographs of candleholders or paintings that are in their trust at various institutions. They are: the Reverend Lockett Ford Ballard, Trinity Church, Newport, Rhode Island; Albert K. Baragwanath and Miss Margaret Stearns, Museum of the City of New York; James Biddle and Miss Mary Glaze, the Metropolitan Museum of Art; John J. Coblentz, the Western Reserve Historical Society; Miss Anna K. Cunningham, the University of the State of New York; John D. Davis, Colonial Williamsburg; Wendell D. Garrett, *Antiques;* Thompson R. Harlow, the Connecticut Historical Society; the Reverend Robert C. Hunsicker, St. Paul's Chapel, New York City; the Reverend Howard P. Kellett, Christ Church, Boston; Mrs. Doris Kershaw, Sandwich Historical Society; James R. Ketchum, the White House; Richard J. Koke, the New-York Historical Society; Rabbi Theodore Lewis, Touro Synagogue, Newport, Rhode Island; Miss Dorothy D. Merrick, Pilgrim Society; L. G. G. Ramsey, *The Connoisseur;* Norman S. Rice, Albany Institute of History and Art; Christian Rohlfing, Cooper Union Museum for the

Arts of Decoration; Miss Rodris Roth, Smithsonian Institution; H. H. Schnabel, Jr., Museum of Fine Arts, Boston; Marvin D. Schwartz, the Brooklyn Museum; Miss Patricia E. Smith and Robert G. Wheeler, Sleepy Hollow Restorations; John A. H. Sweeney, the Henry Francis du Pont Winterthur Museum; M. W. Thomas, Jr., New York State Historical Association; Charles C. Wall, the Mount Vernon Ladies' Association of the Union; and David B. Warren, the Museum of Fine Arts, Houston.

PHOTOGRAPHIC CREDITS: The following individuals and institutions are gratefully acknowledged for having taken or supplied the photographs used in this book: Abby Aldrich Rockefeller Folk Art Collection, 131; Albany Institute of History and Art, 13, 14, 64; Gilbert Ask, 17, 21, 22, 23, 32, 34, 38, 45, 46, 49, 53, 56, 65, 68, 69, 73; Brooklyn Museum, 90, 92, 107, 108; City Art Museum of St. Louis, 39; Colonial Williamsburg, 15, 26, 57, 58, 60, 72; the Connecticut Historical Society, 27, 28; Cooper Union Museum, 109; the Corcoran Gallery of Art, 79; the Corning Museum of Glass, 74, 75, 76; Henry Curtis, 24; the Detroit Institute of Arts, 128, 129; the Dicksons, 4, 5; Mrs. Edsel B. Ford, 19; Frick Art Reference Library, 124, 127; Colonel Edgar W. Garbisch, 63, 125; J. A. and R. H. Glenn, 43; Harvard University, 16; Le Bel's Studio, 62, 77; Mrs. Nina Fletcher Little, 87, 88; Lloyd's Studio, 91; Wally McFall, 105; James Ellery Marble, 44; Haydon Mason, 83, 84, 85, 86; the Metropolitan Museum of Art, 10, 11, 30, 52, 54, 70, 101; the Mount Vernon Ladies' Association, 40, 41, 42; Museum of the City of New York, 31, 33, 47, 55, 96, 97; Museum of Fine Arts, Boston, 9, 25, 48, 78, 99, 100, 114; Museum of Fine Arts, Houston, 6; Museum of Modern Art, 133; the Newark Museum, 98, 126; the New-York Historical Society, 80; Old North Church, 23; Paris-Morris, 18, 61; Phillips Studio, 136; Thurman Rotan, Frontispiece, 1, 2, 3, 7, 12, 29, 36, 50, 51, 59, 71, 81, 93, 94, 95, 102, 104, 106, 110, 111, 112, 117, 118, 119, 120, 121, 122, 123, 130, 132, 134, 135; Abbie Rowe, 66, 67; Elroy Sanford, 37, 82, 89; Shaker Community, Inc., 115; Smithsonian Institution, 113, 116; Touro Synagogue, 35; Malcolm Varon, 20; Yale University Art Gallery, 8; Louis B. Young, 103.

Contents

List of Illustrations

Preface

It is hoped that this work will give a clear picture of the stylistic development of candleholders in chronological progression during the period when these devices saw their greatest flowering in America. The author has included only examples in descriptions and illustrations whose marks indicate their American origin or those that have a basic documentation of ownership and use here. By thus limiting the materials, it is possible to exclude the vast number of antique candle-burning fixtures which have been imported from Europe during the twentieth century. Hopefully, this limitation will provide stronger and more accurate guidelines for furnishing old American rooms with appropriate candleholders.

Included with each period discussed are contemporary American paintings of interiors that show candleholders in place. These, more than any other source, provide information concerning the number of candle fixtures used in rooms and their disposition. In the beginning the paintings present a simple (sometimes naïve) statement of what the artist actually saw; toward the end of the nineteenth century, when antiquarianism was on the rise, the painter often included candleholders of an earlier period in interior views and still-life groupings. Contemporary advertisements also give a valuable record of taste, and when these have been available they are shown. From the early nineteenth century the greatest attention began to be focused on lamps and their various burning fluids. During this period of scientific exploration, candleholders continued to be produced even though their importance was diminished.

An attempt has been made to show and discuss all types of candleholders, whether they stand on the floor or on tables, or hang from the ceiling. It is natural that high style development can best be traced in silver candlesticks because of the precious nature of the basic material; careful attention has been given to this area. Less sophisticated candle fixtures are included in chronological order with more elaborate city-made pieces so that the filtering-down of style can best be studied. If any types of candleholders of which the reader is particularly fond are not found here, it is because the author could not find enough basic documentation of American use for their inclusion.

Dobbs Ferry, New York

J. T. B.

Chapter *1*

Candles and Candlemaking Methods

No EXACT HISTORY OF THE CANDLE IS KNOWN, for its origins are almost as ancient as the history of man. The earliest ancestor of the true candle, the type known today, was the torch. Primitive torches, which are related to the open fire, might be of the simplest and most naturalistic type. They could be made from such materials as a pine knot, a dried tree branch, wood splinters bound as bundles, the body of a small fish or bird, or any other organic material with sufficient flammable content. For purposes of terminology, such lighting devices intended for outdoor use might be called torches; if intended for indoor use, they should be called elementary candles.

One of the most familiar types of elementary candle is the pine-splinter torch. This is made from a splinter or sliver of resinous wood, which is then ignited. Closely related is the rushlight, for which the basic flammable ingredient is the pith of a marsh rush that has been dipped in grease or fat. The coated rush is fastened into a scissors-like holder, generally of iron, and ignited.

The immediate ancestor of the true candle is the taper—a cord that has been thinly coated with fat or wax. When a group of cords that have been treated in this manner are tied together, they are referred to as a "flambeau."

While true candles certainly might have been developed

1

earlier, there is documentary evidence to show their existence by the eleventh century. From this date is preserved a part of the Exultet Roll that is now in the Vatican Library. An illumination from this source shows a tall Paschal candle being lighted from a taper. Several other illuminations from the same roll, which date from the twelfth century, show both large Paschal candles and small candles in use. Despite the fact that candles may have existed in Roman times, the fact remains that they did not come into general use until the fourteenth century. Medieval candles were either carried in the hand or held on pricket, or spiked, stands made of iron, brass, or bronze. A thin metal spike was inserted in the bottom of the candle, and it was thus held in place.

The true candle is formed from a cord or wick surrounded by a thick layer of tallow or wax that serves as fuel. It is, of course, the flame that is the most important part of a burning candle. The candle flame is actually a body of gas in different stages of combustion. The part nearest the wick is a core of unignited gas; this is surrounded by an area where the carbon in the fuel causes the flame to radiate the most heat and light. The third part of the flame is around and above this; here the carbon is being completely oxidized, and vanishes.

Candles were generally made from two types of material— tallow and beeswax. Those made from natural beeswax burned with a more pleasant odor and generally gave off a more stable light. Particular types of beeswax were valued over others for the odor that was given off when they were burned. Beeswax candles were always a greater luxury, and were used almost exclusively in church ceremonies where there was additional symbolic significance. The principal source for tallow candles is the fat extracted from beef and mutton. Because the melting point for both of these is lower than that of beeswax, tallow candles easily bend or melt. While tallow may be extracted from virtually any animal, the mixture of beef and mutton tallow is generally regarded as the most successful.

Another source that yielded basic fat for candles was the bayberry. These shrubs grew abundantly in the American colonies, and the early settlers had often been familiar with them in their homelands. The berries were harvested in the fall and placed in a kettle of boiling water. As the wax rose to the top, it was skimmed off and strained. This process was repeated again and again until a cake of bayberry wax was eventually formed. It was then necessary to melt this cake before candles could actually be produced. Enormous amounts of bayberries were required to produce a single pound of wax. Though bayberry candles were considered better than those made of tallow, they were inferior to beeswax candles. They were probably the most familiar type in use in colonial America.

Much experimentation has gone into finding substitutes for costly beeswax. Bitumen and pine resin were among the earliest substances employed, but the candles produced were still of inferior quality. The first really successful substitute was discovered in the middle of the eighteenth century; it was spermaceti, a substance that was separated from the oil in the head of the sperm whale. Candles made from spermaceti proved to be superior to all others.

However, the decline of the whaling industry brought to an end the supply of spermaceti. Stearine was the next substitute used for candlemaking. About 1815, the French chemist Michel Eugène Chevreul (1786–1889) discovered that animal fats are glycerides. By 1823 he had developed a method for extracting glycerine from tallow to produce stearine. By the mid-nineteenth century a process was discovered that made it possible to produce stearine in large quantities, but it was not perfected until the end of the century. Stearine candles burn with a clear, smokeless flame, and do not bend when exposed to warmth.

The powerful rival to stearine was paraffin wax, which was being produced as early as 1850. Petroleum, when refined by distillation, yields a number of products, of which paraffin is one. Paraffin candles burn with a brilliant white flame that is of greater intensity than stearine. The one disadvantage is that paraffin bends when exposed to heat, and the candles are not suited for use in warm climates. However, if the paraffin is combined with stearic acid or vegetable wax, this defect is corrected. Paraffin eventually became the chief material for candlemaking, and today most candles are made of it.

Wicking for candles can be made from several substances. Primitive types were made from rushes and from tow, which is the coarse part of flax or hemp after it has been separated. The silk from milkweed could be twisted into a simple wick, though it had to be twice the desired length of the candle so that it could be given thickness by doubling it. A straw of rye or oats was often placed in the center of the wick to offer an air space and thus improve the combustion. Because of its low melting point, a tallow candle required a thick wick, while a wax candle required only a thin one. Originally all wicks were twisted; it was not until the early nineteenth century that wicks began to be plaited.

In Europe candlemaking was considered a trade, and was regulated by the apprenticeship system. In London the craft was divided into tallow and wax chandlers, another indication of the important distinction made between these two types of candles. In the American colonies the craft was primarily associated with the home, and was generally considered to be work for women. Wax chandlers also traveled from house to house to assist the housewife in her candlemaking duties.

In general, candlemaking methods can be divided into two basic types—one in which the wax is *applied* in some manner around the wick, and the other where the wax is *molded* around the wick. The first type has four distinct variations that might be employed.

Candle dipping is probably the most ancient, and was for centuries the most commonly employed. The method involves dipping the wick into molten wax or fat, pulling it out, letting it dry, and then repeating the process (Plate 1). Any given diameter can be achieved for the candle, and much practice is necessary to achieve an end product free from lumps. Frames of wood or metal were developed that allowed a number of wicks to be dipped at the same time. Some of these frames were elaborate, and contained several rows of rods for suspending the wicks. Closely related is the method of pouring; here the wax is poured onto the wick. The amount that adheres is allowed to harden; then more wax is poured on. Wax that is partly hardened is sometimes applied to the wick in a process called "building up." This is a highly laborious project, and requires great skill. Drawing is the final method in which the wax or fat is applied to the wick. It is fairly well restricted to the manufacture of long church tapers. The wick is soaked and is then drawn through holes of increasingly large size so that a cylindrical shape can be achieved.

Candle molding eventually became the most universally accepted method because of the ease of production and the fact that more candles could be made at one time. It is thought that the Sieur de Brex first introduced candle molding in Paris in the fifteenth century. A candle mold could contain any number of tubes ranging up to several dozen (Plate 2). The molds vary in length and diameter, and were made of tinned sheet iron, pewter, iron, pottery, and even glass. The wick, after being doubled, was knotted at the end of the tube and was held in a taut position by a stick at the top of the mold (Plate 3). The wax was then poured into the mold around the wick and was allowed to harden. To extract the candles from the mold it was necessary to cut the wicks away from the rod holding them in position and then plunge the mold into hot water. The candles were taken from the mold and then allowed to "season" for a period of several months. This gave them an added hardness so that they burned evenly.

Candles have always been considered a luxury, and today they probably remain the most expensive form of illumination. Candle ends were carefully saved in eighteenth- and nineteenth-century America for use in bedrooms and servant rooms or to be melted for the production of additional candles. While many attempts have been made to simulate it, there is still no substitute for the kind of light given by a burning candle.

1. Dipping beeswax candles. Here the rod, the doubled wick, melted wax, and type of kettle used in candlemaking can be seen clearly. These candles have been dipped about ten times. *Sleepy Hollow Restorations*

7

2. Candle mold, tinned sheet iron, American, c. 1825. This eight-tube candle mold was a possession of the Van Cortlandt family of Croton-on-Hudson, New York, and represents the type most commonly used during the late eighteenth and nineteenth centuries. Height 10⅜ inches.

Sleepy Hollow Restorations

3. Candle mold filled with wax. This twelve-tube candle mold has had the wicking tied at the extremity of the tubes; a stick holds the wicks away from the wax at the top. *Sleepy Hollow Restorations*

Chapter 2

The Baroque Period

✎ *c. 1650-1715*

FIRST, A FEW WORDS CONCERNING DEFINITIONS AND TERMI-
NOLOGY are in order. For the purposes of this work, the word
"candleholder" is used to refer to any object whose primary
function it is to hold a candle in place. There are two devices for
doing this—a socket or a pricket. A socket is a cup or receptacle
into which the candle can be fitted, while the pricket is a spike
that is forced into the center of the bottom of the candle to
hold it in place. The latter category has not been found to be
applicable to documented American candleholding devices, although some might certainly have been used here. Some students
of lighting use "candleholder" to mean a low saucer type of
device that is portable, and "candlestick" to denote a higher-
standing device whose purpose is generally more stationary. Because this distinction seems needless, it is not used here.

"Candleholder" is, therefore, used to describe a great number of different devices. If intended for one candle, "candlestick" is used; if for more than one, "candelabrum" or, plural,
"candelabra." If the device is intended to hang from the ceiling,
and if it has a central shaft and arms, it is called a "chandelier";
or it is called a "lantern" if the candle socket is inside an outer
framework. "Lantern" is also used to define portable lighting

devices enclosed by frames. When models that stand on the floor are discussed, the term "candlestand" is used. And, finally, the term "sconce" refers to a candle-burning device that is affixed to the wall, to an object designed for wall use and containing candleholders, or to candleholders on a piece of furniture. Sometimes "candle branch" or "arm" is used but these are more properly called "sconces."

Candleholders can be made from virtually any material—metals and alloys, pottery, porcelain, enamel, glass, wood, and sometimes even stone. Of course, the material often determines the elaboration of form and design the candleholder takes. Some of the most elaborate have been made from precious and fine metals, glass, and porcelain. The overall satisfaction the finished product gives is determined by the skill with which the craftsman handles the material.

The same general terminology defining the parts of a candlestick applies to other candleholders. The candlestick has a "base" that rests on the floor or a piece of furniture, a "shaft" that rises above the base, and a "candle cup," or "socket," that is used to hold the candle in place. Sometimes a removable member is placed inside the socket or around it; this is called a *bobèche*. Seventeenth-century candlesticks often contain a disk placed around the shaft; this is called a "drip pan" or "drip catcher." The drip pan gradually disappears with the greater refinement of style during the eighteenth century.

Since candleholders are a basic category of the decorative arts because of their important function, they reflect the styles in favor as well as furniture or any other form does. Silver, because of its precious nature, often reflects changes of style and taste before other materials. Therefore, silver candlesticks are an important key to the style of each succeeding period.

The first candlesticks that can be associated with America are in the Baroque style. This style is characterized as being rather heavy and massive, with turning, sometimes in a spiral twist, as an important element of design. The turnings of the spiral twist are intended to give a contrast of dark and light, or "chiaroscuro."

It was the English treatment of the Baroque style that was most influential in America. Therefore, the American candlestick can best be understood in relationship to its prototype. Stylistically, the English candlestick of about 1640 has a base that resembles an inverted cup, and a plain cylindrical shaft with a socket that looks like a spool fixed on the top; the rim of the socket becomes the drip pan. In 1660, the Restoration brought about a revival of interest in Gothic design, and a number of domestic candlesticks were made that show the influence of medieval architecture. These candlesticks are typified by a square molded base crowned by a molded collar from which a shaft formed of eight small clustered (engaged) columns rises. The columns are arranged in a square with one at each corner and one in the middle of each of the four sides and a molded band halfway up the shaft. The top of the shaft (column) is also molded (Plate 8).

The column remained a popular candlestick form throughout the remainder of the seventeenth century. However, the Greek Doric column replaced the Gothic in popularity. In this type the molded collar at the top of the base develops into a protruding boss decorated on the upper side with gadrooning, a band of which also adorns the octagonal base (Plate 9 and Plate 10). Candlesticks of this type generally ranged in height from about six to nine inches. By the end of the century the popularity of these columnar sticks had begun to wane in England. Some of this loss of popularity undoubtedly lies in the fact that the columns had to be hammered entirely by hand, and were therefore difficult and costly to make. Because casting became a familiar process by 1700, another form, which was easier to produce, succeeded the columnar sticks. While these English styles were the ones that were transmitted to America, there was generally a time lag in the development of the style here. Hence, the dates of similar American candlesticks are slightly later.

What is thought to be one of the earliest candlesticks used in America was excavated in 1930 at the site of the Aptucxet trading post in Bourne on Cape Cod, Massachusetts. This trading post was one of three established by the Pilgrims. The one at Bourne was founded in 1626 and was not abandoned until about 1660. The excavated candlestick is made of a type of brass called "latten" that is often mentioned in seventeenth-century New England inventories. It has a saucer base that holds the socket, and a long-shaped handle with a hole in it for hanging; in general, it might be said to resemble a frying pan. Candlesticks of this type were made in both England and Holland. The origin of this stick is not known. It might have been brought from either Holland or England by the Pilgrims or could have been acquired through trade with New Amsterdam. In any case, the stick certainly dates no later than 1660. It is not illustrated here because it is in bad condition and is generally atypical of other candleholders found in use. It is preserved by the Bourne Historical Society, where it can be seen.

Also associated with the Pilgrims are two English candlesticks, one brass, the other pewter, that are preserved at Pilgrim Hall in Plymouth, Massachusetts (Plate 4 and Plate 5). All the ingredients of the Baroque style are typified here in the heavy feeling of the whole and the turning seen on the shaft. These candlesticks were made by casting, with further refinement through turning. However, since the placement of the drip pan near the base of the shaft indicates that one of these candlesticks dates from the mid-seventeenth century and the other slightly later, it seems unlikely that they could have come on the *Mayflower* in 1620. However, they have been associated with the Pilgrims for many years, and were undoubtedly in use quite early in America.

Mrs. Nina Fletcher Little has prepared an important paper entitled *References to Lighting in Colonial Records* (see Bibliography). Wills, inventories, personal letters, diaries, and advertisements provide an invaluable picture of the numbers and uses of candleholders in colonial houses. Much of the material of this nature that is included below is taken from Mrs. Little's study. The conclusions of her paper show that candles were the most often mentioned method of lighting but that even in wealthy homes there were few references to lighting devices.

The Reverend Francis Higginson (1586–1630), who was the first minister in Salem, Massachusetts, in 1628 wrote a letter of advice for settlers who were coming to the New World that listed items that should be brought with them. One of the items he listed was a "lanthorn," which he says could not be otherwise obtained. This early spelling reminds us that polished horn was used for the windows in early lanterns. The inventory of the estate of John Dillingham, who died at Ipswich, Massachusetts, in 1636, does not list candlesticks, but an old dark lantern hanging by the fireplace is mentioned.

In 1652, the inventory of Captain Bozone Allen, who was a Boston shopkeeper, lists one dozen wire candlesticks. Other inventories have similar listings. This probably refers to twisted wire or iron sticks that are generally regarded as European today; but it shows that they were imported at an early date. Captain George Corwin died in Salem in 1684 and left what was for that period a large estate. Listed in the inventory are "looking glasses with brases" in the "old Hall" and "kitchen chamber." These are undoubtedly sconces with candle arms attached to them (Plate 13), and would have been found only in the wealthiest houses. The Reverend Nathaniel Rogers of Ipswich had "4 brasse candlesticks" listed for his kitchen.

Generally, references to pewter candlesticks are not so common as references to brass ones. The will of Thomas Wells of Ipswich in 1666 states that "I give unto my son John Wells, one of the great pueter candlesticks with the top thereof." An invoice survives in the Massachusetts Archives of goods sent from John Caxy of London in 1693 to his agent Joseph Mallenson in Boston; it includes "Three Pr. of new fashioned candlesticks at 3 and 4 s. Two pr. round ditto, 2 s—10 d." (See Plate 6 and Plate 14.) Silver is not mentioned in the records of Essex County, Massachusetts, before 1681. However, a silver candlestick is mentioned in the inventory of William Paine of Boston in 1660.

Mrs. Little also examined a sampling of records from Virginia and New York. In 1653 Stephen Gill died in York County, Virginia, and left the enormous estate of £33,000. Included were seven servants who were worth almost £4,000. However, only a small dark lantern was listed for the "Hall" and three brass candlesticks for the kitchen. The records of New York reveal a larger number of types of candleholders than those of New England or Virginia. Included during the seventeenth century are lanterns, candlesticks (some silver), branched standing candlesticks, sconces (Plate 12), arms on the wall and chandeliers hanging from the ceiling (Plate 13). It is only natural that some of the surviving documented examples should be Dutch (Plate 7).

It is through the known Baroque silver candlesticks that the best clues to contemporary indigenous taste and its influences can be determined. From Boston are candlesticks by the silversmiths Jeremiah Dummer (1645–1718) and John Noyes (1674–1749). (See Plate 8 and Plate 9). The pair by Dummer closely follows English prototypes of about 1666–1670. The heavy stepped base and clustered column are the earmarks of this period. The candlesticks from the end of the seventeenth century by Noyes that have a rounded fluted column are inspired by the London style of about 1680. Thus, English prototypes were highly influential in New England.

Cornelius Kierstede (1675–1757) was a New York silversmith who left behind important examples of his work (Plate

10 and Plate 11). Because of his Dutch background, Kierstede reflects the heavier treatment of the Baroque style that is typical of Holland. The heavy stepped base is elaborately engraved with arabesques, and the fluted column terminates in a highly ornate socket. The snuffer stand that accompanies the Schuyler family candlesticks is made even more Baroque in design by the presence of a double-headed eagle. These three objects were made about 1705. The elaboration of the snuffer stand indicates the importance attached to such an object. Snuffers could be of the scissors type that would trim the wick (used in this kind of stand). If of a conical shape that merely extinguished the flame, they are called "douters." Snuffers, spelled "snofors," usually of brass, are occasionally listed in seventeenth-century inventories.

The period from about 1650 to 1710 witnessed the importation of candleholders from Europe, as well as the beginnings of crafts in America that turned to making them. In general, surviving candleholders that can be documented are quite rare, and early records indicate a considerable scarcity of lighting devices in households.

4. Candlestick, brass, English, c. 1650. Old tradition states that this candle-stick was brought from England in 1620 on the *Mayflower* by William White, the father of Peregrine White. The style of the candlestick, especially the placement of the drip pan, suggests the style of the mid-seventeenth century, and this would tend to discount the tradition. However, the candle-stick has long been identified with the possessions of the Pilgrims; therefore it has been in the United States for many years. Height 6 inches.

Pilgrim Hall

5. Candlestick, pewter, English, c. 1670. Traditionally, this candlestick also has Pilgrim associations. It is said to have been brought by the group of settlers who arrived on the *Anne* under the leadership of Edward Winslow in 1624. However, the style is suggestive of a later date. There is probably some substantiation for the use of this candlestick in early New England, for it has long been among the Pilgrim possessions. It bears the engraved monogram "$W^{B}_{\ L}$." Height 6¼ inches.   *Pilgrim Hall*

6. Candlestick, pewter, York, England, William Allen (working 1667–1674) c. 1670. This candlestick was brought from England by the Buell family of Connecticut. Deacon John Buell was the leader of a group of settlers who moved from Wethersfield to Litchfield in 1719. It was acquired in the present century by Mrs. Katharine Prentis Murphy from Dr. Charles Turkington of Litchfield, who had acquired it from the Buell family. Height 7 inches. *The Museum of Fine Arts, Houston; The Bayou Bend Collection*

7. Candlestick, brass, probably Dutch, c. 1675. The Baroque spiral twist is fully developed in the shaft of this candlestick. The grotesque engraved on the base with surrounding foliage is also indicative of Baroque design. The candlestick was found in New Paltz, New York, and has a long history of ownership by a Huguenot family there. Height 11½ inches.

Sleepy Hollow Restorations

8. Pair of candlesticks, silver, Boston, Jeremiah Dummer (1645–1718), 1686. These silver candlesticks are probably the earliest of American make that survive. The shaft of eight clustered columns is another Baroque device often seen in English and Continental candlesticks of the mid-seventeenth century. They were made for the marriage of David Jeffries and Elizabeth Usher in 1686. Marked "I" over "DE" with engraved arms of Jeffries, Usher, Clarke, and Everard or Lidgett families. Height 10¾ inches.

Yale University Art Gallery; Mabel Brady Garvan Collection

9. Pair of candlesticks, silver, Boston, John Noyes (1674–1749), 1695–1700. The Baroque influence here is to be seen in the fluted column with stopped reeding. These candlesticks were made for the Bowdoin family, and are engraved with that crest. Height 9¼ inches.

Museum of Fine Arts, Boston; gift of Miss Clara Bowdoin Winthrop

10. Pair of candlesticks, silver, New York City, Cornelius Kierstede (1675–1757), c. 1705. These candlesticks are extremely elaborate for their early date. The shaft is composed of a fluted column with stopped reeding. The square base terminates in the shaft and is engraved with grotesques and further embellished with gadrooning. The type of decoration suggests Dutch influence. The candlesticks were made for John and Elizabeth Schuyler and are engraved with an "S" over "IE." Height 11¾ inches.

11. Snuffer stand (below, in center), silver, New York City, Cornelius Kierstede (1675–1757), c. 1705. The snuffer stand held the scissors-like snuffers that were important in trimming the twisted wicks of candles. This was made to go with the candlesticks shown in Plate 9. The rectangular stepped base is engraved with grotesques; an embossed bulbous stem supports a rectangular box embossed with a double-headed eagle displayed. It is engraved "S" over "IE" for John and Elizabeth Schuyler. Height 8 inches.

The Metropolitan Museum of Art

12. Sconce, tinned sheet iron, probably Hudson River Valley, 1704. This sconce represents a more provincial treatment of the Baroque style. It was found in the Hudson River Valley by the late Stephen Van Rensselaer and was published by him in an old *Antiques* article (see Bibliography). The date "1704" would appear to be contemporary with the other embossed decoration on the sconce. The pineapple or tree design at the top and embossed hearts are well conceived. Height 18 inches.   *Sleepy Hollow Restorations*

13. *Belshazzar's Feast,* oil on canvas, anonymous painter, probably Albany County, New York, first quarter of the eighteenth century. The so-called "Patroon painters" recorded in their canvases members of the Hudson Valley aristocracy of the early eighteenth century, as well as biblical scenes. The source for this painting is probably an engraving from the Van Rensselaer family Bible, which was printed in Holland in 1702. While the lighting fixtures shown are Dutch in origin, they are an interesting survival of Baroque forms in an American painting. The chandelier is probably one of the type with a ball at the base of the shaft with arms extending from it. The presence of the two grotesque figures is highly unusual. Over the doorway is a kind of lantern that contains two burning candles, and a candle arm has been attached to the Baroque looking glass at the right. On the table are two low candlesticks of the type popular in Holland in the seventeenth century.

Albany Institute of History and Art

25

14. *Christ at Emmaus,* oil on wood panel, anonymous painter, probably Albany County, New York, first quarter of the eighteenth century. Another religious Patroon painting that has no known source, it too may be based on a print or drawing that was probably Dutch, to judge by the costumes. The table holds two low Baroque candlesticks with round bases and elongated sockets. *Albany Institute of History and Art*

Chapter 3

The Queen Anne
and Chippendale Periods
 ❧ *1715 - 1780*

THE QUEEN ANNE AND CHIPPENDALE PERIODS are treated as
a unit here for stylistic convenience and continuity. The chief
difference in the styles, as they relate to candleholders, is the
application of Rococo ornamentation, during the Chippendale
period, to what is essentially the rounded Queen Anne form.
Only in ornamental detail does the form change.

As has been stated, it was improvements in methods of
metal casting during the late seventeenth century that helped
to change the form and design of candlesticks. The usual method
used for casting candlesticks was to make a model in wax and
to prepare a hinged iron mold from this. The metal was heated
to a liquefied state and then poured into the mold where it was
allowed to cool. The candlestick was then removed from the
mold and cleaned and finished on a lathe. Ornaments in relief,
such as those associated with the Rococo style, were cast separately and applied to the candlestick. Candlesticks produced by
this method were solid.

In the 1690's a process was developed in which the shaft
could be cast hollow. Separate vertical halves were made and
then joined together, invisibly, leaving the center hollow. Silver

was generally employed in this method and there was, of course, a considerable saving of metal. The process was far less costly and time-consuming than fashioning the silver by hand, as was done with columnar candlesticks. Although it was desirable that the parts be imperceptibly joined, a fine line generally can be seen. Cast sockets can usually be distinguished by the presence of one or two ribs around the circumference.

Other changes also took place during the Queen Anne period. Earlier, candlesticks were rarely made in numbers more than matching pairs. Now, in England, it became customary to make them in double pairs, and by 1730 even this number was increased to sets of a dozen. American candlesticks generally remained low, but some English models increased in height to as much as twelve inches.

Queen Anne silver and brass candlesticks were both generally hollow-cast. In brass sticks the shaft is hollow throughout, and the end protrudes through and is separate from the base, the two being so carefully brazed together from within that no dividing line can be seen. This is one of the most reliable methods for identifying brass sticks of the period, as any other method of fastening the shaft to the base leaves a well-defined line.

Both silver and brass candlesticks of the Queen Anne type have common characteristics. Both are made from a high quality of metal—silver often having a lesser alloy content than sterling; and the brass was of a bright yellow color with a soft texture that takes a high polish. An excellent standard of casting and finishing existed for both metals at the time. The base of the candlestick might be round, square, hexagonal, or octagonal in a low, flat treatment of the inverted cup form. The shaft is conceived in a pure baluster form whose turnings might vary from the rounded true baluster to a kind of mushroom-shaped knob. The socket is waisted, and has no flange above it; any semblance of the drip pan completely disappears. In general, the lines of Queen Anne candlesticks follow those of all the other decorative arts of the period. Delicacy, daintiness, and curved lines and surfaces dominate. The earlier Queen Anne sticks are distinguished through their square, hexagonal, and octagonal bases that are a holdover from the heavy, rigid lines of the Baroque period (Plate 15 and Plate 16). As the eighteenth century progresses, this squaring-off disappears and more rounded lines become dominant (plates 17, 18, and 19).

The French Rococo style was introduced to English silversmithing in the late 1720's, although it was not generally popular until about 1735. Metal provided an excellent medium for this elaborate ornamentation because it made possible the reproduction in sharp detail of such typical motifs as C-scrolls, masks, shells, and other naturalistic devices. By 1740 some English candlesticks began to be burdened by such ornament, and many surviving examples have a grotesque quality. The overall lines of the Queen Anne stick are retained, although there are several significant changes. The base often has four or six highly accented, rounded corners; sometimes a shell is used at each corner. The shaft becomes thinner and often has more exaggerated turnings in the baluster; a separate *bobèche*, or drip cup, fits down into the socket, and often has edges that repeat the design of the base. For some unknown reason this fully developed Rococo or Chippendale style does not seem to have been very popular in America, as few examples of it survive (plates 20, 30, 31, and 33). This can perhaps be attributed to a lack of technical knowledge regarding the casting process. As a matter of fact, this could be the reason for the great scarcity of American silver candlesticks from the eighteenth century. It is interesting to note that included in the inventory of the silversmith John Coney's (1655–1722) estate is a reference to "2 candlestick molds." The account books of Paul Revere (1735–1818), which cover a thirty-six-year period between 1761 and 1797, reveal the name of only one client, Zachariah Johonnot, among

over five hundred for whom candlesticks were made. The entry
of 1762 reads:

A pr of Silver Candlesticks	
wt 45 oz 17 at 7/	£16–0–11
To the Making	£ 8–0–0
To a Pr of Snuffers and Snuf dish	
wt 12/6/6	
Making Snuffers	£ 1–4–0
Making Snuf dish	£ 2–8–0

The following year an entry records another pair of sticks of
a lighter weight for the same client.

Brass candlesticks were seldom marked either in England or
in America. At this time so little is known about brass making
in colonial America that it is difficult to attribute any candlesticks to this country. A few sticks have come to light that have
a documented history of ownership here, but it can only be
speculated as to whether they are English or American (Plate
32). While pewter was not very popular in England at the time,
several candlesticks by American pewterers survive; these provide important documentary evidence because they are generally marked (Plate 34). It was during the eighteenth century
that many varieties of candleholders came into use in American
homes. Chandeliers of brass and glass were imported from England for use in churches, public buildings, and private resi-
dences. Brass chandeliers had a turned center shaft generally
terminating in a ball or series of balls. The arms could extend
from the shaft at one or more places. The number of tiers of
arms determined the importance of the chandelier (Plate 23
and Plate 24). This was the period when the great glass houses
of England and Ireland were producing highly ornate table
candlesticks and chandeliers. The early glass chandeliers (about
1740) generally had a heavy center shaft that was faceted. From

this, candle arms extended to terminate in sockets that usually rested on a glass *bobèche,* which was further embellished with prisms. The long strings of glass beads extending from the canopy to the socket are identified with the late eighteenth and early nineteenth centuries. In 1719 the *Boston News Letter* carried the advertisement "Lately imported from London, fine glass lamps and lanthorns, well gilt and painted, both convex and plain being suitable for halls, staircases, and other passageways, to be sold in Glass Shop in Queen St." In 1724 Governor William Burnet of New York had a mansion in which the hall was lighted by a large lantern with three lights. In one room "2 branches for 3 lights" are mentioned, while in another he had "2 large brass sconces with glass arms."

By the mid-century the previously mentioned spermaceti candles had become popular. The *Boston News Letter* of March 30, 1748 carried the advertisement:

> To be sold on Minot's T. by James Clemens, Sperma Ceti candles, exceeding all others for beauty, sweetness of scent when extinguished; Duration being more than double tallow candles of equal size; Dimension of the flame nearly four times more, emitting a soft, easy, expanding light, bringing the object close to sight, rather than causing the eye to trace after them, as all tallow candles do. One of these candles serves the use and purpose of 3 tallow ones, and upon the whole are much pleasanter and cheaper.

Two other forms of candleholders that gained great popularity were sconces and candlestands. The inventory of 1736 of the estate of the Philadelphian Patrick Gordon, who had been governor of Pennsylvania, listed ornate and expensive branches and sconces; and advertisements from newspapers of this period frequently mention "A variety of sconces with branches, in walnut frames with gilt edges." Sconces with backs made from quillwork encased in a glass frame were popular. Branches of silver or glass were attached to the frame, and the flame of the candle was reflected in the glass (Plate 21 and Plate 22). Inventories and wills also mention "brass ball, iron candlesticks," which must refer to the candlestands of these materials, which were often made in New England (plates 25, 26, 27, 28, and 29). The standard was of iron, and the candle cups, drip pans, and a finial at the top were generally brass. Since candlestands of this type were also made in England, it is difficult to distinguish American examples unless they are marked.

Not all American candleholders were directly influenced by London fashions of the day. Indigenous craftsmen used wood and tinned sheet iron to great advantage. Some of the lanterns, sconces, candlestands, and chandeliers made by local craftsmen show a complete mastery of a craft as well as an ingenious interpretation of prevailing style. A completely regional character is revealed in many of these creations (Plate 36 and Plate 37).

Two contemporary pictures provide an interesting glimpse of how candlesticks were disposed on tables. The earlier of these (about 1754) is George Roupell's *Mr. Peter Manigault and His Friends;* three sticks with Chippendale bases are casually placed among the other table accessories, with no definite plan of arrangement (Plate 38). Similarly in John Greenwood's *Sea Captains Carousing in Surinam* of 1758, the disposition of the candles is casual, even chaotic. From their round bases and baluster-shaped shafts these sticks would appear to be Queen Anne. These candlesticks reflect in one manner the eighteenth-century idea that furnishings were of a movable nature, and should be changed in the room as occasion demanded. The furniture form known as the "candlestand" was a small table that could be picked up and moved beside a chair where a candlestick could be placed on it. Thus, the use of candlesticks within rooms gives a good insight into manners and customs of the day.

15. Pair of candlesticks, silver, Boston, Edward Winslow (1669–1753),
1715–1720. The faceted base presents a greater elaboration over the plain
octagonal base; the stem is baluster-turned. The maker's mark, "EW" with
a fleur-de-lis, is enclosed within a shaped shield on the exterior of the base,
and there is an unidentified crest of a winged unicorn opposite the maker's
mark. These are very similar to a pair of candlesticks by John Coney (1656–
1722) that were a tutorial gift to Henry Flynt of Harvard College in 1716.
These candlesticks are not illustrated here, but they presently belong to Henry
N. Flynt of Deerfield, Massachusetts. Height $7\frac{1}{16}$ inches.

Colonial Williamsburg

16. Pair of candlesticks, silver, Boston, John Burt (1692/3–1724). The faceting of the octagonal base is reduced to a splayed octagon. They were presented to Nicholas Sever, a tutor at Harvard College from 1716 to 1728. They are marked "I. Burt" in a cartouche and are engraved "Donum Pupillorum 1724." Height 7 inches.   *Harvard University*

17. Candlestick (one of a pair), silver, Boston, Nathaniel Morse (1685–1748), c. 1720. The curved line and greater delicacy of the Queen Anne style are reflected in this candlestick. The octagonal base and bulbous turned shaft are also indicative of the early development of this style. Arms of the Faneuil family are engraved on the left side of the base, and on the opposite side is the later Caulfield crest with the motto "Deo Duce Ferro Comitante"; "NM" is impressed in a rectangle. Height 6⅛ inches.

The Henry Francis du Pont Winterthur Museum

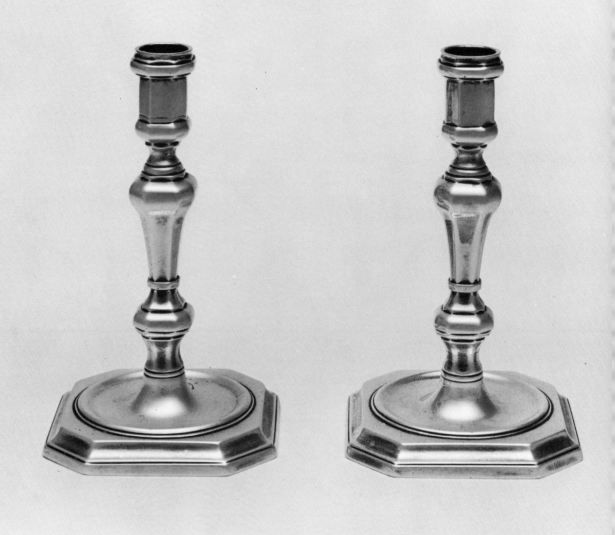

18. Pair of candlesticks, silver, New York City, Adrian Bancker (1703–1772), 1724–1740. The octagonal bases in this pair of candlesticks have an irregularity of sides that has previously not been observed. The bases plus the turned bulbous shaft are extremely successful together as a design unit. They are marked "AB" twice in an oval under the foot. Height $7\frac{1}{4}$ inches.

Mr. and Mrs. Samuel S. Schwartz

19. Pair of candlesticks, silver, New York, Charles Le Roux (1689–1745), c. 1730. In this model, the octagonal splayed foot has cut corners and supports an octagonal baluster stem. The candlesticks are marked "CLR" conjoined in an oval, and are engraved with a female figure holding a mask and an anchor and the initials "SS." Height 6½ inches.   *Mrs. Edsel B. Ford*

20. Pair of candlesticks, silver, New York, Simeon Soumain (c. 1685–c. 1750), c. 1735. These candlesticks have an elaborate stepped base that is more complicated than many of the Queen Anne models. This elaboration anticipates the oncoming Rococo style. The candlesticks are shown, together with appropriate furnishings, in the owners' country house on the Eastern Shore of Maryland. Height 7 inches.

Colonel and Mrs. Edgar W. Garbisch; courtesy The Connoisseur

21. Quillwork sconce, silver candle arms, Boston, Knight Leverett (1703–1753), c. 1728. Quillwork was a fashionable pastime for young ladies during the first half of the eighteenth century. It was made from twisted quills of colored paper that were decorated with mica and adorned with wax figures. The entire construction was placed in a frame with glass, and a candle sconce was often attached. The mica of course caught the light and provided an interesting reflection through the glass. The drip pans are engraved with the letter "R" for Ruth Read, the wife of John Read, a lawyer who eventually settled in Boston. Marked "K. LEVERETT" in a shaped rectangle. Length of arm: 7⅛ inches.   *The Henry Francis du Pont Winterthur Museum*

22. Quillwork sconce (one of a pair), silver candle arm, Boston, Jacob Hurd (1702–1758), 1729–1740. The candle arm is hinged to the backplate so that it can be pivoted. These sconces were owned by Parson and Mrs. William Smith of Braintree, Massachusetts; their daughter Abigail married John Adams. Marked with "HURD" in a rounded rectangle. Length of arm: 4¾ inches. *The Henry Francis du Pont Winterthur Museum*

23. Chandelier, brass, English, c. 1724. This twelve-light chandelier, which is one of a pair, was acquired by the Old North Church of Boston from England in 1724 and installed on January 6, 1725; it is the earliest surviving chandelier in America. On the basis of the similarity of the candle sockets to a chandelier at Stogursey, Somerset, England, Charles Oman, in an *Antiques* article (see Bibliography), has attributed the chandelier to John Bailey of Bridgwater, Somersetshire. The bird on the top of the central shaft is often seen on English chandeliers of this period. *Old North Church*

24. Chandelier, brass, English, 1728. The inscription "Thomas Drew, Exon, 1728" undoubtedly refers to the Exeter bell founder of the same name. It is original to Trinity Church in Newport, Rhode Island. This is one of three chandeliers that are original to the church, but this is the only one that is inscribed. *Trinity Church, Newport, Rhode Island*

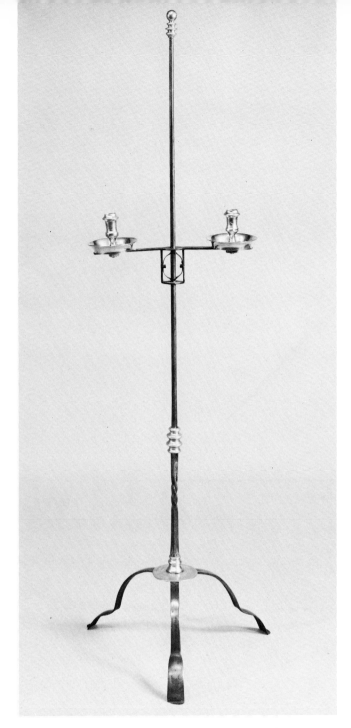

25. Candlestand, wrought iron and brass, Boston, B. Gerrish, c. 1736. Candlestands of this type were made both in New England and in England. Through a type of spring device, it is possible to adjust the height of the double candle arm. The sockets are generally supported by deep drip pans. Stamped "B. GERRISH" in brass drip pan. Height 49½ inches.

Museum of Fine Arts, Boston

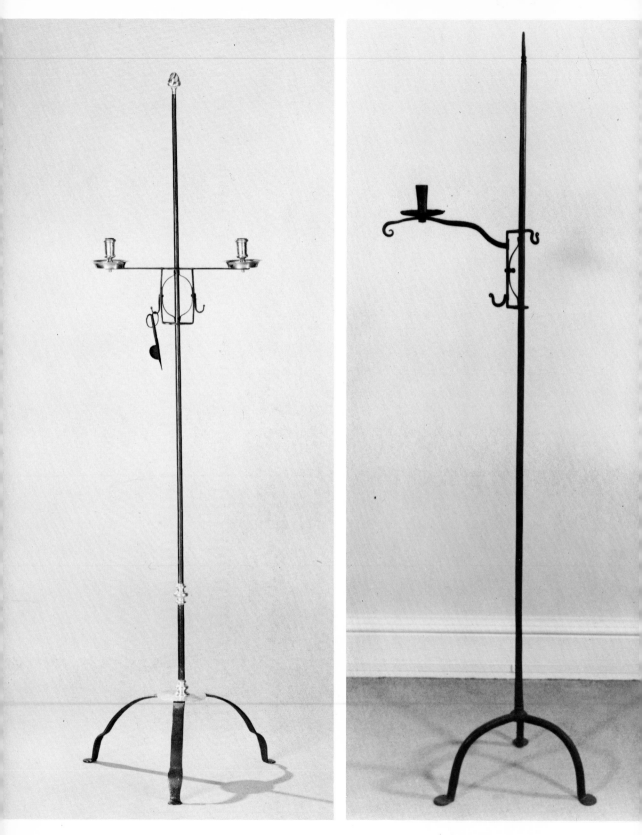

Opposite, left

26. Candlestand, wrought iron and brass, New England, c. 1740. This closely resembles the documented example by B. Gerrish. Because of its stylistic resemblances to the documented example and an old New England history, it is probably safe to call it American. A pair of iron snuffers hangs from an accessory hook. Height 68 inches.   *Colonial Williamsburg*

Opposite, right

27. Candlestand, wrought iron, probably English, c. 1751. This simplified candlestand has only one candle arm and is made completely of iron. It was owned by Colonel Elisha Williams of Hartford, Connecticut. Height 41¾ inches.   *The Connecticut Historical Society*

28. Detail of preceding plate, showing the spring action that allows the candle arm to be adjusted in height; two accessory hooks are also seen.
The Connecticut Historical Society

29. Candlestick, brass, English, c. 1740. A striking resemblance to the brass candle fittings on candlestands can be seen in this small candlestick. The candle cup can be unscrewed from the base to ensure its use in traveling. It was owned by the Van Cortlandt family of Croton-on-Hudson, New York. Height 2 inches. *Sleepy Hollow Restorations*

30. Pair of candlesticks, silver, Boston, Jacob Hurd (1702–1758), c. 1740–1750. A slightly different treatment of the standard Queen Anne form is seen here, as well as a tendency toward the Rococo. Hurd may have cast these sticks from a French mold. It is of interest that Hurd also made the candle arm on the quillwork sconce shown in Plate 21. Height 6¼ inches. *The Metropolitan Museum of Art*

Opposite

31. Candlestick (one of a pair), silver, New York City, William Anderson, c. 1750. The beginnings of the Rococo or Chippendale style are to be observed in this example. The stepped base has curved cut corners, and the shaft tapers from the top to the bottom. The initials "M" over "NM" are engraved on the shaft for Nathaniel and Mary (Crooke) Marston, and the mark "HB" conjoined in an oval is stamped in the base. Height 7¼ inches.

Museum of the City of New York

32. Candlestick, brass, probably English, c. 1750–1775. Here the full Rococo or Chippendale style is developed. The base is now composed of seven lobes or petals; the turned shaft has a tapered section under the candle cup, and a *bobèche* is provided. The candlestick was owned by Mrs. Elizabeth Lewis Bell (1760–1848) of Little Creek Landing, Kent County, Delaware. Height 10 inches.

The Henry Francis du Pont Winterthur Museum;
gift of Dr. Margaret I. Handy

33. Candlesticks, silver, New York City, Samuel Tingley (working in New York 1754–1767, in Philadelphia 1796) c. 1765. The Rococo style is included in most of the details of these sticks. Tingley was one of the few American makers who embraced the style completely. Height 10 inches.

Museum of the City of New York;
gift of Mrs. Eton Huntington Hooker

34. Candlestick (one of a pair), pewter, Lancaster, Pennsylvania, Johann Christopher Heyne (1715–1781), c. 1752–1780. This candlestick is a great rarity because of its American make; it closely resembles European altar candlesticks. It was probably made for a Jesuit church, and is engraved "IHS" surmounted by a cross on the base, a cross on each side opposite this, and above is a plaque that is engraved "IN/RI." It is marked "ICH" in a shield below "LANCASTER" in a rectangle. Height 21¼ inches.

The Henry Francis du Pont Winterthur Museum

35. Interior of Touro Synagogue, Newport, Rhode Island. The synagogue was designed by the architect Peter Harrison (1716–1775) and erected in 1763. The chandeliers are contemporary with the building. The large center chandelier is Dutch in origin; it is brass, and dates c. 1750. The two smaller brass chandeliers (of a set of four) are English in origin, and date about 1740. The large candlesticks are brass, probably of English origin, and date from the early nineteenth century.

Society of Friends of Touro Synagogue National Historic Shrine

36. Lantern, tinned sheet iron painted red, New England, c. 1765. The lantern, of hexagonal shape, has freestanding finials at the top of each of its sides, which resemble leaves. An almost identical lantern is preserved at the Bostonian Society Museum in Boston, Massachusetts. Tradition associates this lantern with the demonstration against the Stamp Act of May 21, 1766, when it is said to have been hung from the northwest bough of the Liberty Tree at Washington and Boylston streets opposite Frog Lane. Hence the name "Liberty Tree" is often applied to these lanterns. Height 21 inches.

Sleepy Hollow Restorations

37. Sconce, tinned sheet iron and mirrored glass, probably Philadelphia, c. 1774. This is one of a set of twelve sconces that were traditionally made by a Philadelphia tinsmith for Carpenter's Hall in Philadelphia; it is believed that these sconces were in place when the First Continental Congress met on September 7, 1774. Two of the sconces are still preserved in Carpenter's Hall. Height 24½ inches. *The Western Reserve Historical Society*

38. *Mr. Peter Manigault and His Friends*, watercolor and ink on paper, Charleston, South Carolina, George Roupell, c. 1754. In this rare painting, from a period in which few American interior views are known, the table contains three candlesticks of the full-blown Rococo or Chippendale type (Plate 31). The casual disposition of the candlesticks, as well as that of the other utensils on the table, is probably quite typical of the mid-eighteenth century. *The Henry Francis du Pont Winterthur Museum*

39. *Sea Captains Carousing in Surinam,* oil on bed ticking, American, John Greenwood (1727–1792), 1758. Here the candlesticks are of the transitional Queen Anne to Chippendale type (Plate 29). The bases are more evenly rounded and have turned shafts. Since they are in use in a tavern, they are undoubtedly of brass or pewter. *City Art Museum of St. Louis*

57

Chapter 4

Neoclassicism

⥀ 1780 - 1810

DURING THE 1760's A NUMBER OF TECHNOLOGICAL DEVELOP-
MENTS OCCURRED in England that completely revolutionized
the production of candlesticks. Chief among these was the bi-
valve process of core casting—now both the shaft and the socket
could be cast in one hollow piece. It was still necessary, however,
to cast the base separately and to join the two together. Previously it had been necessary to hammer by hand in the process
of making a sheet of silver. Now processes were developed that
made this feasible by rolling. These industrial processes per-
mitted a reduction in the amount of metal required to make a
candlestick.

Pressing and stamping processes were so well developed that
by the mid-1780's a master silversmith could purchase individual parts of a candlestick that had been made previously and
assemble them by soldering into a well-composed stick. It was
at this time that a process originated that made it possible to
apply a thin sheet of metal over copper. Thermomechanical in
its application, the silver attached itself to the copper by a kind
of fusion. Birmingham and Sheffield became important centers
of this trade, the latter being so influential that the term "Sheffield plate" is often applied to this kind of material.

It was also discovered that candlesticks produced from very thin sheets of solid silver could be weighted with a mixture of powdered pumice and resin; this was generally placed in the base of the stick to give it stability. Later in the century, probably about 1790, it became possible to roll the silver into still thinner sheets, and lead was placed in the base of candlesticks to weight them.

By 1770 Neoclassicism was firmly entrenched in English design. It was a style primarily fostered by Robert Adam (1728–1792), and took its inspiration from the ornamentation of Roman and Renaissance monuments. Extreme delicacy of ornamentation and symmetry characterize this style. The baluster shaft for candlesticks was completely superseded, and vertical lines came to dominate. The columnar shaft again came into popularity, especially in the form of the Corinthian order, which was often liberally interpreted by designers of the day (Plate 50). Delicate festoons of drapery or flowers, urns, masks, rams' heads, and other classical motifs began to be applied to candlestick surfaces in low relief or engraving.

The base of candlesticks of this type was usually formed by a stepped foot which was often a high four-sided pyramidal pedestal supported by a series of two or three square-faced steps. The sides of the base were usually ornamented in low relief with acanthus leaves, floral swags, or rams' heads. Gadrooning was often used, in addition, on the edges of the steps. The fluted column rested on this base and was crowned by a capital that might also be decorated with swags or other classical devices. The socket generally contained a loose *bobèche* that stylistically followed the lines and ornamentation of the base.

Another popular candlestick type that was a variation on the true columnar type became popular in England in the 1770's and 1780's. Here the shaft had four flat faces tapering downward and terminating in a base that was often quite similar to the pedestal base of the true columnar form. Sometimes, however, the base was oval, rounded off, hexagonal, or octagonal (Plate 40). Invariably the socket of this type was shaped like an urn, and generally contained a removable *bobèche*. In the late 1780's this form was further modified so that the shaft became rounded (still tapering downward); the shaft was often fluted vertically or in a diaper pattern (Plate 46 and Plate 51) in a well-defined manner. The urn shape with flaring edge was still retained for the socket, and a round loose drip pan was inserted under it. All these forms were popular until the end of the eighteenth century. While in its fullest and most elaborate development the Neoclassic style can be best defined in silver candlesticks, brass, copper, bronze, and pewter were also used, although naturally it was not possible to secure as much delicate detail in these materials.

The Neoclassic style became popular with American silver-smiths in the 1780's. Some of the craftsmen who created the most successful indigenous sticks were Joseph and Nathaniel Richardson (working about 1771–1791) in Philadelphia (Plate 48), Joseph Lownes (working 1780–1816) of the same city (Plate 52), Daniel Van Voorhis and Garret Shanck, who were partners in New York in 1791 (Plate 47), Isaac Hutton (working 1800–1825), Robert Shepherd and William Boyd (partners in 1810) of Albany, New York (Plate 54 and Plate 55), and John Lynch (1761–1848) of Baltimore (Plate 49). Each of these men, in his own way, provided a unique interpretation of English Neoclassicism.

American-made silver snuffers are extremely rare, but since the greatest preponderance of those that survive date from the Neoclassic period, it might be well to say a word about them. They ranged in size from about four to six inches in length. The blades were held closed by a coil spring that was usually concealed by a boss in the hinge. The smaller examples were supported on one foot under the box; larger examples had three feet—one under the box and one under each of the handles. The feet raised the snuffers off the tray so that they could easily be grasped. The box was used to catch the wick when it was clipped off. Generally snuffers were plain, with their excellence of design depending on a careful handling of the line of the handles (Plate 53); in a few examples the box was engraved with delicate Neoclassic detail (Plate 47).

Especially popular at this time were low saucer-base candlesticks, which were often called chambersticks. These invariably had a ring handle so that they were easily portable, and are often associated with bedroom use (Plate 41 and Plate 55). Sometimes these were equipped with glass shades, and silver douters were made to go with them. An interesting variation on this idea is the candle tray containing snuffers and a douter by Joseph Lownes (Plate 52). This example is not well designed, for it is evidently made from a tray that was intended to hold only a snuffer; and a snuffer and a douter have been placed on either side of an oversized socket.

English candlesticks continued to be popular in America after the Revolution. This is well illustrated in the home of George Washington, who had English plated candlesticks and lamps at Mount Vernon in the 1780's (Plate 40 and Plate 41). English glass also remained in demand, and was imported in considerable quantities. The candelabra and chandeliers of the late eighteenth century usually contain delicate swags of glass beads draped in a Neoclassic manner (Plate 42 and Plate 43). Churches became important clients for glass chandeliers, which were often imported for this specific use (Plate 44 and Plate 45).

The American craftsman continued to produce candleholders of a more simple style in tinned sheet iron and wood. Popular in country inns and churches were chandeliers with a turned wooden shaft and tinned sheet-iron arms (Plate 56 and Plate 57). While the effect is completely different, Neoclassic lines are nonetheless often retained. Sometimes tinned sheet iron alone was used to fashion candleholders, and the effect achieved can be very fresh and exciting (Plates 59, 60, and 61). Candle-stands made of wood replaced in popularity those made of brass and iron (Plate 58). These were generally made adjustable by the presence of a screw-turned shaft.

A few delightful primitive pictures that show Neoclassic interiors (Plate 62 and Plate 63) survive from the early nine-teenth century. While it is generally impossible to distinguish exactly the type of candlestick in use, the severe lines of Neo-classicism are always evident.

40. Pair of candlesticks, silverplate on copper (Sheffield plate), English, c.
1783. These candlesticks are considered to be a part of the original furnishings that George and Martha Washington acquired for Mount Vernon. A
cash memorandum dated November, 1783, survives, with the entry "By 4
pr of Plated Candle Sticks a $2\frac{1}{2}$ Guins pr pair." It is thought that these
candlesticks are a pair of the four mentioned. Their linear severity and use
of such devices as swags, beading, and acanthus leaves are all typical of the
Neoclassic style. Height $10\frac{1}{2}$ inches. *The Mount Vernon Ladies' Association*

41. Chamber candlestick, silverplate on copper (Sheffield plate), English, c. 1783. Such small hand candlesticks as this were used on desks and in bedrooms because of their portable nature. This may be one of the candlesticks mentioned in the Mount Vernon cash memorandum of November, 1783, where an entry reads "By 2 pr. flatt ditto [candlesticks] with snuffrs." These traditionally belonged to George and Martha Washington. The shape of the candle socket and gadrooning around the *bobèche* and base are Neoclassic motifs. Length 3⅛ inches. *The Mount Vernon Ladies' Association*

42. Pair of candelabra, glass and brass fittings, English, c. 1789–1790. Candelabra of this type were made extensively in the British Isles at the end of the eighteenth century; they are closely related in style to chandeliers. The use of a prism crowned with a canopy as the central shaft and festoons of glass beads opposite the two candle arms is Neoclassic. These are a part of the furnishings of Mount Vernon, and are considered property of the Washingtons. Height 25 inches. *The Mount Vernon Ladies' Association*

43. Candelabrum (one of a pair), glass and brass fittings, English or Irish, c. 1785. This is quite similar stylistically to the pair shown in Plate 42. The flattened side with protruding candle arm opposite probably indicates that this candelabrum was conceived to be used on a mantelpiece or against a wall. The candelabra were a part of the furnishings of the Schuyler Mansion near Albany, New York, and were acquired during the occupancy of the house by Philip Schuyler. Height 26¾ inches.

New York State Historic Sites

44. Chandelier, glass and brass fittings, English or Irish, c. 1802. The vestry minutes of St. Paul's Chapel, New York City, for December 13, 1802, state: "Ordered that the Committee of Leases and Repairs provide three suitable Chandeliers for Trinity Church and a Set of Chandeliers for St. George's and St. Paul's Church." This is one of that original set for St. Paul's Chapel of which thirteen presently survive. The central shaft and canopy with festoons of glass beads extending to the candle arms is typical of the late Neoclassic period. *St. Paul's Chapel, New York City*

45. Chandelier, glass, Venice, c. 1790. Of unusual interest in America, this Venetian chandelier was presented by Lady Selina Huntingdon in the 1790's to the Prospect Street Church in Newburyport, Massachusetts, where it remained until the present century. The elaborate treatment of the glass branches is typical of the glass made in Venice.

The Henry Francis du Pont Winterthur Museum

46. Pair of candlesticks, silverplate on copper (Sheffield plate), English, c. 1785–1810. The inverted helmet shape of the candle cups, and the tapered shafts and oval bases, are all Neoclassic design elements. They are engraved with a crest identical to the device used by the Latimer family of Wilmington, Delaware. It consists of a heraldic wreath surmounted in a dexter arm in armor embowed, holding in the hand a dagger bent in sinister. The candlesticks are from the house of Dr. Henry Latimer in Wilmington, and the inventory of his estate made on April 26, 1820, lists similar candlesticks. Height 11 inches.

The Henry Francis du Pont Winterthur Museum

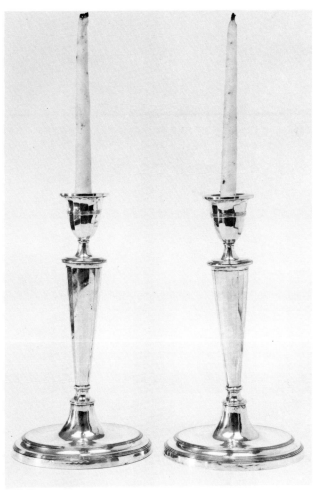

47. Candle snuffers, silver, New York, Daniel Van Voorhis and Garrett Schanck (partners, 1791), c. 1791. Elaborate Neoclassic drapery and festoons are engraved on these scissors-type candle snuffers. The engraved script initials "MT" are for a member of the Thurston family of New York. Snuffers of this type were often accompanied by a tray, which is missing in this example. Length 6¾ inches. *Museum of the City of New York;*
gift of Miss Mary Thurston Cockcroft

Opposite
48. Pair of candlesticks, silver, Philadelphia, Joseph and Nathaniel Richardson (working c. 1771–1791), c. 1785. These sticks have molded square bases with gadrooned bands and fluted columns with molded top and bottom. They are engraved with script "MB" on the base and are marked "I. NR" in a rectangle. *Museum of Fine Arts, Boston;*
gift in memory of Dr. George Clymer by his wife, Mrs. Clymer

71

72

49. Candlestick (one of a pair), silver, Baltimore, John Lynch (1761–1848), c. 1795. It is interesting to compare this candlestick with the English examples shown in Plate 40. Here much of the Neoclassic refinement of detail is lost, although the overall line is certainly the same. The mark "I. L" in a rectangle is impressed on the side of the square base. Height $9\frac{1}{8}$ inches.

The Henry Francis du Pont Winterthur Museum

50. Pair of candlesticks, silverplate on copper (Sheffield plate), English, c. 1800. Simplification and a coarsening of detail characterize these candlesticks. They are typical of the type that began to be mass produced in the English factories during the early nineteenth century. This pair belonged to Washington Irving, and are a part of the original furnishings of his home, Sunnyside, at Tarrytown, New York. They were probably acquired in England by Irving. Height $8\frac{5}{8}$ inches.

Sleeepy Hollow Restorations

74

51. Pair of candlesticks, silverplate on copper (Sheffield plate), English, c. 1800. Again, as in Plate 49, there is a coarsening of Neoclassic detail. The festoons and acanthus leaves do not become a part of the overall design, but rather seem to be superficial detail. These candlesticks belonged to Washington Irving, and were probably purchased in England; they are a part of the original furnishings of Sunnyside at Tarrytown, New York. Height 7⅛ inches.

Sleepy Hollow Restorations

52. Candlestick, silver, Philadelphia, Joseph Lownes (working 1780–1816), c. 1800. This is a type of candlestick intended for use on a desk. The tray could serve as a receptacle for writing equipment as well as for the snuffers and douter. However, the candle socket is of the same size as that which would be found on a standing candlestick. Hence, the proportions are wrong and the whole has a squat look. Height 5⅛ inches.

The Metropolitan Museum of Art

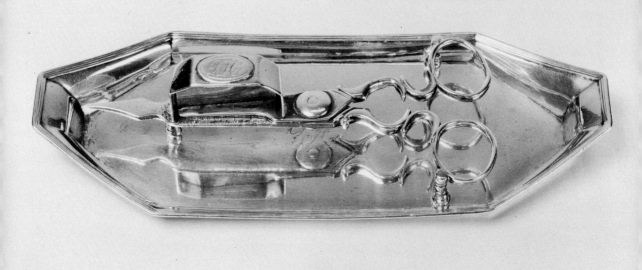

53. Candle snuffers and tray, silver, Charleston, South Carolina, Daniel Carrel (working 1790–1806), c. 1800. Daniel Carrel worked with his brother John in Philadelphia and then alone in Charleston. It is thought that these snuffers were made during his Charleston period. It is engraved "DH" in script for one of the Hart family of Massachusetts, and is impressed with the mark "CARREL" in a rectangle. Length of snuffers 6½ inches; length of tray 8⅞ inches.   *The Henry Francis du Pont Winterthur Museum*

54. Pair of candlesticks, silver, Albany, New York, Isaac Hutton (working 1800–1825), c. 1815. Here is a continuum of the Neoclassic stick with column support is to be seen. The statement is very simple, and the result quite pleasing. Height 7 inches.   *The Metropolitan Museum of Art*

77

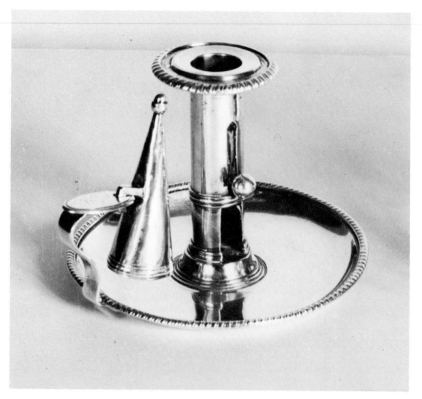

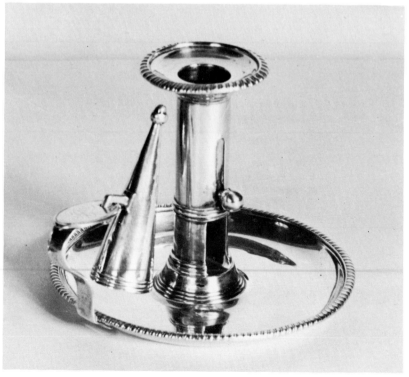

55. Pair of chamber candlesticks, silver, Albany, New York, Robert Shepherd and William Boyd (partners in 1810), 1814. Conical candle snuffers called "douters" are attached to the thumbpieces of each of these chamber candlesticks. They are initialed "AS" in script for Ann Stevenson who became the second wife of Pierre Van Cortlandt II in 1813. A bill of sale dated 1814 accompanies this pair. Height 4⅜ inches.

Museum of the City of New York; bequest of Joseph B. Brenauer

56. Chandelier, white pine and tinned sheet iron, Massachusetts, c. 1790–1810. The bulbous turned wooden shaft retains simplified Neoclassic lines; into it are secured six candle arms. Chandeliers of this type were often used in churches or public buildings. Height 16½ inches.

The Henry Francis du Pont Winterthur Museum

57. Chandelier, white pine (painted dark brown and gilt), iron, and tinned sheet iron, New England, late eighteenth century. There are sixteen candle arms attached to this chandelier, which is a more elaborate version of the one shown in Plate 56. It is one of seven originally used in a New England church. Height 25 inches.   *Colonial Williamsburg*

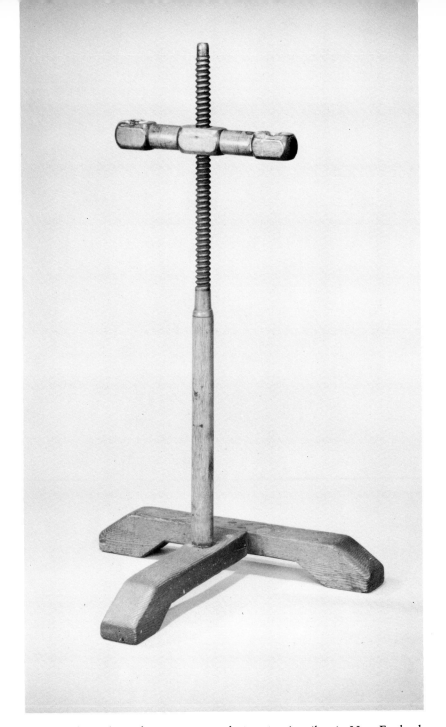

58. Candlestand, maple (crossarm), ash (post), pine (base), New England, late eighteenth century. Candlestands of this type often have a highly refined functional beauty. The post is screw-turned so that the height of the crossarm with candle sockets can be adjusted. New England appears to be the area in which most of these were made. Height 30¼ inches.

Colonial Williamsburg

59. Lantern, tinned sheet iron painted red, probably Connecticut, late eighteenth century. While this lantern is of a purely functional form, the decoration at the top and openwork scallops provide a pleasing effect. The lantern was found in Connecticut and traditionally has a long history of ownership there. Height 10 inches. *Sleepy Hollow Restorations*

60. Chandelier, tinned sheet iron with traces of gold paint, probably New England, late eighteenth or early nineteenth century. The proportions of the Neoclassic style are maintained in this primitive piece. The fluted candle saucers are typical of the period, and are often found on New England pieces. Height 26½ inches. *Colonial Williamsburg*

61. Hanukkah light, tinned sheet iron, probably New England, late eighteenth century. Hanukkah lights are a considerable rarity when they are American and date from such an early period. They were used for the Jewish Festival of Lights, which lasts for eight days with one candle lighted each succeeding day. Hence, there are eight candle sockets and an additional one, called the *shamash*, or "server"; this was used for lighting the candles. It has been speculated that this Hanukkah light might come from the area around Ipswich, Massachusetts. Height 11 inches.   *Mr. and Mrs. Samuel Schwartz*

62. *Two Women*, watercolor on paper, Connecticut, Eunice Pinney (1770–
1849), c. 1810. Neoclassicism as it filtered to more provincial areas is to be
noted in many of the details in this drawing, that is, drapery treatment, floor
covering, costumes. The single lighted candlestick is of a completely Neoclassic type, with the inverted helmet-shaped candle socket and tapering shaft
(Plate 46).   *New York State Historical Association*

THE COTTERS SATURDAY NIGHT

63. *The Cotters Saturday Night*, watercolor on paper, Connecticut, Eunice Pinney (1770–1849), c. 1815. The single burning candlestick is not so easy to define stylistically as that in the drawing by the same artist in Plate 62. However, it would appear that this is a more primitive type, probably made of tinned sheet iron. It is also possible that it might be a candlestick of a much earlier form that was still in use (Plate 5), although no drip pan is evident.   *Colonel and Mrs. Edgar W. Garbisch*

Chapter 5

The Federal Age

⮜⮞ *1810 - 1845*

THE DAWN OF THE NINETEENTH CENTURY saw the emerging new Republic anxious to place herself beside the other major nations of the world. This happened not only in politics but also in the arts. The emphasis shifted from England to France as the source to which American designers turned for inspiration. The French Empire style, which was popular at the time, tended toward a more literal or archaeological interpretation of Classicism. Now there was a desire actually to reproduce objects associated with classical antiquity, not merely to apply classical surface ornament.

Candleholders began to be greatly influenced by this style, which in England was called Regency. An extremely popular object for wall decoration and lighting was the girandole looking glass. Generally crowned by an eagle or some other Empire device, the mirror frame was round, enclosing a convex or flat piece of glass. At the bottom was a drop that completed the design, also generally a classical device. At either side of the glass, candle arms were often placed; these allowed the light to be reflected and doubled through the mirror image (Plate 64).

Americans of means were anxious to import French lighting fixtures for their homes. The official designers for Napoleon were Charles Percier and Pierre F. L. Fontaine, who together published in Paris in 1812 *Recueil de Décorations Intérieures*. . . . This work contained many designs for lighting fixtures which were ornamented with the sphinx, caryatid, eagle, acanthus leaf, and a wide range of other classical ornaments. In Paris the firm of Paul-Philippe Thomière was probably the best known for the production of these bronze and ormolu candleholders (Plate 67). Denière et Matelin was another Parisian firm from which documented examples exist in the United States (Plate 66). Indeed, when President James Monroe was refurbishing the White House in 1817, candelabra were ordered from both firms.

An important French innovation of the early nineteenth century was the development of the *bouillotte* light. This was a candelabrum, generally with several branches, which had a circular flaring shade attached to a central shaft over the candle flame. The shades were made of tinned sheet iron, brass, copper, and silver. Since American brass founders were quick to make their own versions of French lighting fixtures, it is only natural that the *bouillotte* light should be among these, and an example survives that bears the label of Baker, Arnold and Company of Philadelphia (Plate 65).

Silver continued to be popular, although bronze was a better medium for casting the heavy ornamentation that was applied to Empire candleholders. In England, candlesticks reflected the tendency for the heavier lines of the Regency. Although Neoclassicism was still represented in the overall form of the candlestick, all its elements took on different proportions. Gadrooning became heavier, and the shaft was conceived as a series of lumpy parts rather than a column (Plate 68). Sheffield plate continued to be popular in England, and remained so throughout the century.

The American silversmith now began to feel the effects of the Industrial Revolution, which had begun much earlier in

England, where it was reflected during the Neoclassic period. Now individual cast ornaments were available to the American silversmith. Some of the candlesticks and candelabra produced at this time show a highly sensitive treatment of the Empire style through the application of classical ornaments (Plate 69). As has been stated, silver quickly reflects, more than any other material, the changing fashions of a period. There exists an amazing pair of candlesticks by the New York silversmith William Thomson (Plate 70). Although these were made about 1825, they are a full embodiment of the Rococo revival style, which did not become popular in furniture forms for another twenty years.

In brass and pewter new candlestick forms began to evolve about 1825–1830. The brass sticks generally had a round base that was arched, a round shaft that was banded, and a heavy urn-shaped socket with removable *bobèche* (colored frontispiece and Plate 71). Fine-cut decoration was freely applied to the surfaces of candlesticks of this type. Pewter candlesticks did not develop in so delicate a form. The base was round; the shaft turned in an exaggerated manner, and a spool-shaped socket with flaring rim completed the piece (Plate 72). Tinned sheet iron also continued to be used, often carrying on the traditions and forms of the late eighteenth century (Plate 73).

By the early nineteenth century the American glass industry was well established not only on the eastern seaboard but also in the Midwest. Many of the free-blown candlesticks that survive from the period (about 1815–1840) have been attributed to glasshouses in the Pittsburgh area (Plates 74, 75, 76). These most often have a round base, a columnar shaft, and an urn-shaped socket with flaring rim. This general form also survives in some Midwestern candlesticks that were made by the blown-in-mold method. (A glob of glass is blown into a shaped iron mold.) While the candlesticks of the Pittsburgh area were generally clear or of one color, these later products from the Ohio glasshouses were sometimes streaked with a number of different colors (Plate 89).

However, the most famous candlesticks of the period are those made by the Boston and Sandwich Glass Company on Cape Cod. It was founded in 1825 by Deming Jarves (1790–1869), who developed the pressing machine that made it possible to mold glass mechanically. The earliest candlesticks produced by this factory were blown-molded and had stepped bases and baluster-shaped shafts (Plate 83). Other candlesticks were made that were completely pressed by machine. It is believed that one of the earliest patterns of this type was the Petal and Loop, which was made in different colors (Plate 84). It is the candlesticks that have figural shafts that are the best known. The Dolphin is probably the most familiar; it was made in different colors and heights, and with modifications in the base (Plate 85). The Caryatid and Crucifix were patterns that also enjoyed widespread popularity (Plate 86). These were made in opaque glass as well as with a frosted shaft in the case of the Caryatid. The New England Glass Company in Cambridge, Massachusetts, was another glasshouse that produced a large number of highly interesting candlesticks in the mid-nineteenth century (Plate 90).

Glass was also employed in the manufacture of chandeliers and hall lamps. The chandelier shape became more classical, its base often resembling a basket, and formed by strings of glass beads (Plate 77 and Plate 81). Another popular type that was based on an English Regency model had large flat disks forming tiers from which prisms were suspended (Plate 80). Hanging hall lights had shades in clear, colored, or opaque glass. Sometimes these were decorated with Empire devices (Plate 82).

Ceramics was another industry that became important during the first half of the nineteenth century. Bennington, Vermont, became nationally known for the pottery and porcelain that was made there. About 1845 Christopher Weber Fenton established Lyman, Fenton and Company; in 1850 the name was changed to United States Pottery Company. Large numbers of candlesticks and lamp bases were made at Bennington. These ranged from standing candlesticks of the columnar type with different types of bases to low saucer-base sticks (Plate 91). The greatest number made was in the dark mottled brown heavily glazed finish that characterizes much of this pottery. A factory for manufacturing soft-paste porcelain was opened in 1847 at Greenpoint in Brooklyn, New York, by Charles Cartlidge. Apparently the output of candlesticks in this porcelain was small, for very few have survived. The extant group follows the lines of typical metal candlesticks of the period (Plate 92).

As has been seen in the other periods covered, the country craftsman continued to produce candleholders from more humble materials. Tinned sheet iron was used to fashion lanterns, some of which had sides that were pierced in fanciful designs. These lanterns have come to be known as "Paul Revere" (Plate 94). Other lanterns had straight lines and were virtually devoid of ornament (Plate 95). A few lanterns survive from this period that are said to have been made by sailors; one very interesting example is said to have been made by a sailor returning from Africa and Polynesia, and the elements of these primitive art forms are to be seen in it (Plate 93).

The Federal period produced some fine native painters. Genre was a favorite theme, and interiors that contained lighting devices were often depicted (plates 78, 79, 96, 97, 98, and 100). The folk tradition also flowered during this period, and many delightful interior views were produced (plates 87, 88, and 97). All these pictures reveal the growing popularity of lamps, which are generally seen in use along with candleholders.

64. Girandole looking glass, white pine with gilt paint, Albany, New York, c. 1805–1810. Looking glasses of this type with attached candle arms were very popular during the Federal period. Many types of ornament other than the eagle served as finials. The candle cups were generally arranged in front of the mirror so that the flame would appear doubled. When the mirror is flat, these looking glasses are generally regarded as American; if the mirror is convex, they are thought to be English. Height 50 inches.

Albany Institute of History and Art

65. *Bouillotte* candelabrum, brass and tinned sheet iron painted, Philadelphia, Baker, Arnold and Company, c. 1804–1814. While candelabra of this type were well known in France in the early nineteenth century, this marked American example is a great rarity. The shade is adjustable by a screw at the top so that the intensity of light given by three candles can be regulated. Height 28 inches. *The Henry Francis du Pont Winterthur Museum*

66. Pair of candelabra, bronze and ormolu, Paris, Denière et Matelin, c. 1817. All the elements of the French Empire style are to be seen embodied in these candelabra. Here there is an archaeological attempt to copy classical antiquity instead of allowing the inspiration of it. These are among the objects ordered from France by President James Monroe during the refurbishing of the White House in 1817. Height $33\frac{1}{2}$ inches.

The White House

67. Candelabrum (one of a pair), bronze and ormolu, Paris, Paul-Philippe Thomière, c. 1817. The front of the base is decorated with Roman trophies in relief and on the sides are laurel wreaths, and a caryatid standing on a sphere supports the candle arms; all these are Empire design elements. These candelabra were also among the objects ordered from France by President James Monroe in 1817 for the refurbishing of the White House. Height 42 inches.   *The White House*

68. Pair of candlesticks, silverplate on copper (Sheffield plate), England, c. 1815–1830. While these candlesticks still retain Neoclassical lines and decorative elements, there is a heavy quality that would not be present in a pair of earlier candlesticks. There is an old tradition that these candlesticks were owned by the painter Rubens Peale. Height 12 inches.

The Henry Francis du Pont Winterthur Museum

69. Candelabrum (one of a pair), silver, Philadelphia, John Owen (active 1804–1831), 1815–1831. This candelabrum has a refinement of Empire detail rarely seen in American silver. The overall effect is completely satisfying, and grace and beauty dominate. It is marked "I. OWEN" in a rectangle on the outside of the base. Height 15½ inches.

The Henry Francis du Pont Winterthur Museum

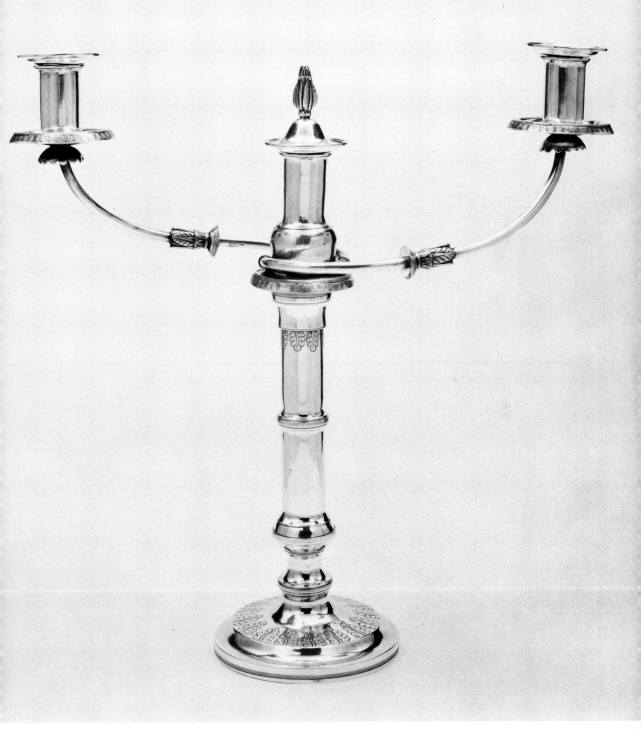

70. Pair of candlesticks, silver, New York City, William Thompson (active by 1810), c. 1825. Since silver has always been regarded as a precious material, it is only natural that objects made of it should be among the first to reflect changing tides of taste. William Thompson is best known for silver that is directly influenced by the Empire style; however, here the candlesticks reflect the influence of the Rococo revival style, which did not become generally popular in the decorative arts until the 1850's. Height 11 inches.

The Metropolitan Museum of Art

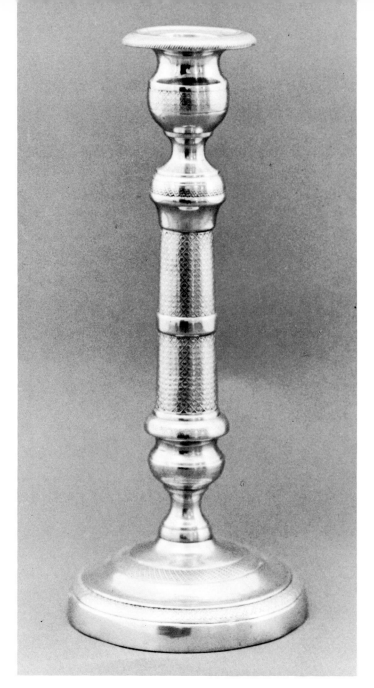

71. Candlestick (one of a set of four), brass, probably English, c. 1825–
1830. The fine-cut decoration on the shaft is another typical feature of the
Empire style. This candlestick has a heavy quality that would not be seen
in an example from the Neoclassical period. The set of candlesticks was
owned by the Van Cortlandt family of Croton-on-Hudson, New York, and
is still preserved in the Manor House there. (See colored Frontispiece.)
Height 8 inches. *Sleepy Hollow Restorations*

72. Pair of candlesticks, pewter, New York City or Poughkeepsie, James Weekes (working 1820–1835), c. 1830. All the lines are rounded in these candlesticks, although they retain the heavy Empire feeling. Sticks of this type in both pewter and brass were often found in American homes of the early nineteenth century. The touch is "J. WEEKES" in block letters on the underside of the base. Height 7½ inches.   *Colonial Williamsburg*

73. Sconce, tinned sheet iron painted, New England, c. 1825. While sconces with oval backs with crimped edges and flattened candle arms are often found in New England, they rarely appear with such elaborate painted decoration. Here, Empire scrolls and a diapered pattern elevate this sconce to a minor work of art. It was found in New England, and is assumed to have been made there. Height 11 inches.

The Henry Francis du Pont Winterthur Museum

74. Candlestick, glass, Pittsburgh area, c. 1815–1830. This candlestick is freeblown with tooled decoration in the baluster. The shaft (baluster) is found with a double hollow air-twist parallel with cobalt blue streaks. Height $11\frac{5}{8}$ inches.   *The Corning Museum of Glass*

75. Candlestick, glass, Pittsburgh area, c. 1820–1840. In this example, which is pattern-molded and free-blown, the glass is purple-blue. The particular form is known as the "pillar." Height 10¼ inches.

The Corning Museum of Glass

76. Pair of candlesticks, glass, probably Pittsburgh area, c. 1830–1840. Again the pillar form is to observed, as in Plate 74 and Plate 75. The glass is clear and is free-blown and pattern-molded. The pillar form relates to the classical column seen also in silver, brass, and pewter. Height 12⅜ inches.

The Corning Museum of Glass

77. *Mrs. William Cooper Seated in Otsego Hall*, watercolor on paper, Cooperstown, New York, "Mrs. Freeman," 1816. This delightful watercolor gives many details of the Federal interior. Of special interest is the chandelier in the center of the ceiling. It is obvious that it is made of glass beads in a kind of basket shape; it has been wrapped in a piece of fine cloth for the summer when it would not be in use. This was a fairly common housekeeping practice during this period.

New York State Historical Association

78. *The Dinner Party*, oil on canvas, Boston, Henry Sargent (1770–1845), c. 1820. Most of the lighting fixtures shown here are oil-burning lamps. However, on the dining table a single Federal candlestick can be seen that closely resembles the type shown in Plate 71 as well as in the Frontispiece.

Museum of Fine Arts, Boston; gift of Mrs. Horatio A. Lamb

79. *The Old House of Representatives*, oil on canvas, Washington, D.C., Samuel F. B. Morse (1791–1872), 1822. The great chandelier that is being lighted in the center of the room is surely an oil or gas fixture. However, on the Speaker's platform is a pair of silver three-branch candelabra that strongly resembles the one shown in plate 69. *The Corcoran Gallery or Art*

80. *Interior of the Park Theatre*, oil on canvas, New York City, John Searle, 1822. Included in the audience are actual portraits of many of the most prominent New Yorkers of the day. The great glass chandelier is quite different in form from those of the late eighteenth century. Prisms now become extremely popular, and the festoons of beads secondary (see Plate 81). The lights seen hanging from the first balcony are oil-burning.

The New-York Historical Society

CHANDELIERS.

BRILLIANT CHANDELIERS, suitable for Public Rooms and Churches, with four, six, eight, twelve, sixteen, eighteen, twenty-four, thirty-two, 36 or 48 Lights, for sale by the subscribers; who have also for sale, either at Wholesale or Retail, a great variety of Cut and Plain Glass, elegant Tea and Dinner Services;— together with a complete assortment of Earthenware, Glass and China.

GEO. DUMMER & CO.

sept 7   31 Pine street.

81. Chandelier, advertisement from the *New York Commercial Advertiser*, September 8, 1824. The advertisements of George Dummer & Co. appear from 1820 until 1825. In the New York directory they are listed as glass and china dealers. It is thought that although the company imported from Europe, it still manufactured a certain amount of glass locally. A George Dummer was the manager of the Jersey City Glass Company that was established in 1824, so it is highly possible that there was a connection between the two.   *The New York Public Library*

82. Hanging lantern, glass (painted) and brass, possibly New England, c. 1830. The white opaque glass is painted with a band of Empire foliage and masks. When the globe is pulled down, a single candle socket is revealed inside. Lanterns of this type were extremely popular for use in halls. Height (shade) $9\frac{1}{2}$ inches.   *The Western Reserve Historical Society*

83. Three candlesticks, glass, Sandwich, Massachusetts, c. 1836–1858. This group of clear flint candlesticks is blown-molded. The baluster shape is still maintained, and there are modifications of the number of steps on the individual bases. Height (left to right) $8\frac{5}{8}$ inches, $6\frac{3}{8}$ inches, $8\frac{1}{2}$ inches.

Sandwich Historical Society

84. Three candlesticks, glass, Sandwich, Massachusetts, c. 1836–c. 1855.
Each of these flint candlesticks is in the Petal and Loop pattern and is pressed
glass. The candlestick at the left is of clear glass; that in the center is colored;
and the example on the right is opaque in two colors.

Sandwich Historical Society

85. Three candlesticks, glass, Sandwich, Massachusetts, c. 1836–c. 1855.
The most familiar of all the Sandwich flint pressed-glass candlestick patterns
is the Dolphin. This group contains all the major types to be found. At the
left is a great rarity in white opaque glass with a scalloped base; the central
example in clear glass is the most ordinary, and has a single stepped base;
while the stick to the right in colored glass has a double stepped base.
Height (left to right) $8\frac{5}{8}$, $6\frac{3}{8}$, $8\frac{1}{2}$ inches.   *Sandwich Historical Society*

114

86. Four candlesticks, glass, Sandwich, Massachusetts, c. 1836–c. 1855. Two more types of pressed flint glass Sandwich candlesticks are to be seen here—the Caryatid and Crucifix. Both of these patterns were very popular and were made at factories other than Sandwich. Each of these examples is of colored or opaque glass, the stick at the far right being extremely interesting because of the frosted surface of the caryatid. Height (left to right) $9\frac{3}{4}$, $9\frac{7}{8}$, $9\frac{7}{8}$, $9\frac{3}{4}$ inches.   *Sandwich Historical Society*

87. *Mr. Russell's Daughter's Bedroom,* watercolor on paper, Philadelphia, Joseph S. Russell, 1853. This delightful watercolor, which is one of a set of ten, shows a pair of blue glass dolphin candlesticks on the dressing table. These are probably of the type shown in Plate 86.   *Mrs. Bertram K. Little*

88. *Mr. Russell's Bedroom,* watercolor on paper, Philadelphia, Joseph S. Russell, 1853. On the mantelpiece two candlesticks are to be seen; both are painted in blue. One would appear to resemble a dolphin form and the other a baluster-stem type.   *Mrs. Bertram K. Little*

89. Pair of candlesticks, glass, Zanesville, Ohio, c. 1840. These sticks are blown-in-mold and are cased on the exterior with clear glass; they are non-flint. The colors of the two differ—that on the right is streaked with shades of yellow, lavender, purple, and white, while that on the left is streaked with light blue, blood red, white, and flecks of gold dust. Height 8 inches.

The Western Reserve Historical Society

90. Candlestick, glass, Cambridge, Massachusetts, c. 1869. Of a highly unusual translucent glass, this pressed hexagonal candlestick was made by the
New England Glass Company. While it still adheres to the columnar form,
it has a heavy quality not found in earlier candlesticks of the same type.
Height 9⅛ inches. *The Brooklyn Museum*

91. Two candlesticks, pottery (flint enamel), Bennington, Vermont, 1849–1858. The saucer-base candleholders have an extremely fine modeling of detail for the Bennington factory. Height (top) $3\frac{1}{2}$ inches, (bottom) $3\frac{1}{2}$ inches.

Bennington Museum

92. Candlestick, porcelain, Brooklyn, New York, c. 1855. Closely adhering to the columnar form often found in brass candlesticks, this example is attributed to the Greenpoint (Brooklyn) factory of Charles Cartlidge. Several candlesticks of this same form have been discovered. Height $9\frac{1}{4}$ inches.

The Brooklyn Museum

93. Lantern, brass and glass, American, c. 1830. This curious lantern has a traditional history associated with the sea, and has been considered a piece of sailor's handiwork. The face reveals a strong African or Polynesian feeling. The chimney can be extended (as shown here) or pushed inside; the front opens on hinges to disclose a single candle cup; the mouth is formed of a glob of glass that acts as a magnifier; two ring handles are attached at the rear so that the lantern can be carried. Height (chimney extended) 8 inches.

Author's Collection

94. Lantern, tinned sheet iron and glass (removed for photograph), Hudson River Valley, c. 1830. The pierced panel on the rounded side of the lantern provides a highly decorative effect when the candle is lighted. Lanterns like this were made throughout the nineteenth century, and are often referred to as "Paul Revere." This is undoubtedly a name that arose during the late nineteenth or early twentieth century for this type. The example shown here was found in the Hudson River Valley and is assumed to have been made there. Height 16¾ inches.   *Sleepy Hollow Restorations*

95. Lantern (one of a pair), tinned sheet iron and glass, Hudson River Valley, c. 1835. Of a completely utilitarian shape, the only ornamentation to be seen is in the perforation that allows the smoke to escape. It was found in the Hudson River Valley. Height 12 inches. *Sleepy Hollow Restorations*

96. *Lecturer and His Audience at Clinton Hall,* ink on paper, New York City, artist unknown, c. 1838. The candlesticks shown on the lecturer's table have round bases with openwork or a decoration in a triangular pattern. They maintain the lines of the Federal period. *Museum of the City of New York*

Reading-room —.

97. *Reading Room,* watercolor and ink on paper, New York City, Nicolino Calyo (1799–1884), c. 1840. On the mantelpiece stands a pair of candlesticks with glass prisms for ornamentation. It is impossible to ascertain the material from which the sticks are made, but they are Federal in their lines.
Museum of the City of New York

98. *Interior of a Butcher Shop,* oil on canvas, American, artist unknown, c. 1840. Against a wall to the left a single tinned sheet-iron sconce can be seen. This is of the rectangular type with a single candle socket and the top of the plate bent out from the wall to catch smoke. (Detail, top.)

Newark Museum; gift of William F. Laporte

99. *Girls' Evening School*, pencil and watercolor on paper, American, artist unknown, c. 1840. Four tinned sheet-iron sconces of the type seen in Plate 98 are in use here. They are supplemented by simple baluster-stem candlesticks that are probably of the "hogscraper" type (see Plate 109).

Museum of Fine Arts, Boston; M. and M. Karolik Collection

100. *Rustic Dance After a Sleigh Ride,* oil on canvas, American, William Sidney Mount (1807–1868), c. 1845. On the mantelpiece are two candlesticks of differing types. The example to the left is the round baluster model (Plate 72), while at the right is a saucer-base candlestick with candle ejector (Plate 110). *Museum of Fine Arts, Boston; M. and M. Karolik Collection*

Chapter *6*

Historical Revivalism and Art Nouveau

1845 - 1900

IN THE 1840's ARCHAEOLOGICAL CLASSICISM began to decline in popularity, and historical revivalism of another sort began to become dominant. Other cultures of the past were explored for their design and ornamentation—the French Bourbon styles, the Gothic and Renaissance periods, Oriental exoticism, and so on. Sometimes there was a desire on the part of a designer actually to reproduce an old object, while at others the ornamental detail was applied to the surface of a completely foreign piece. Sometimes elements from a number of cultures were incorporated into a single piece, and eclecticism resulted. By the end of the century design influences were often so disparate that it was impossible to tell what the designer originally had in mind.

Candleholders felt three major influences during the second half of the century—first, the influence of historical revivalism on high-style candleholders; second, the development of simple standard candleholders that could be mass produced and used in a humble manner; third, at the end of the century, the complete break with revivalism called Art Nouveau. These will be covered in this order. It is also to be remembered that during this period candleholders were often conceived in a decorative rather than a utilitarian sense. Great improvements were being made in lamps through new wicks and the development of new burning fluids—kerosene came into use during the Civil War. Gas was also an important illuminant for interiors and outdoors. Because people still liked the soft glow of a candle flame, candleholders continued to be produced.

Probably the most familiar candleholders from the nineteenth century are the mantel sets that were generally called "girandoles." These often consisted of a center candelabrum with three or more sockets and a pair of candlesticks for use on either side. They were invariably cast of brass, which was given a gilt finish, and had cut prisms suspended from an oval or round ornament under the socket. The bases were usually marble, and the shaft could be of a great variety of patterns (plates 101, 102, and 103). Probably the two greatest producers of these girandoles were Cornelius and Co. in Philadelphia and Dietz, Brother & Co. in New York (Plate 104). The shafts reflected the influence of the Louis XV (Rococo) revival, the Gothic revival, and many other eclectic elements.

Other types of candleholders showed the influence of historical revivalism. Sometimes these were candlesticks in which several different revival tendencies were incorporated; at other times extremely elaborate candelabra were so weighted with ornamentation and glass prisms that it was virtually impossible to distinguish the different elements (plates 106, 107, and 108). Surely candelabra of the latter type were made only for their ornamental impact. During the 1870's and 1880's catalogs of the great international exhibitions reveal the extent to which eclecticism had gone. Classical figures often supported candle sockets of completely different sources (plates 118, 119, and 120). Chandeliers and sconces were possibly the most ill-conceived of all candle fixtures, being completely weighted down with historical ornament (Plate 121 and Plate 130).

The other group of candleholders that was being produced simultaneously was of a much humbler type. Probably the most universal candlestick of the century was the "hogscraper" (Plate 110 and Plate 115). It was made of tinned sheet iron; the base was a round disk with sharp edges, the shaft a cylinder of metal with a flaring rim at the top for a socket. Sometimes they were provided with a candle ejector and a hook for hanging, and were further ornamented by bands of brass or iron around the shaft. The name is derived from the idea that the edges of the base could be sharpened and used to clean a hog in butchering. Many problems are involved in dating these sticks. It is thought that they were in use in the late eighteenth century and continued through the nineteenth. Some examples are stamped "SHAW," but these were probably made at Birmingham, England, for export to the United States. It has been impossible to document any hogscraper for use in the United States before 1853. Hence, the example with patent stamping is included, although contemporary paintings reveal that they were in use much earlier.

Second in popularity of use was the saucer-base candlestick also made of tinned sheet iron (plates 111, 112, and 113). The large round saucer had a socket soldered in its center and a ring handle that made it easily portable. Conical douters were occasionally provided as well as an ejector in the socket; sometimes the stick was painted. These were made throughout the century. An interesting page from the catalog of the Dover Stamping Company in Boston, which is dated 1895, shows the variety of these sticks, which could still be obtained at that late date (Plate 113).

The second half of the century saw a craze for inventing candleholders that could be patented. As has been seen, the hogscraper (Plate 110), a form that had been in existence for many years, was given a patent in 1853 based on "Construction of Iron Candlestick." Folding pocket lanterns became popular at this time, and many patented types were developed (Plate 116). These were small tin cases in which a candle stub and matches could be carried. The presence of mica windows made it possible to convert the case into a lantern that could be used when traveling. Parades were very popular, especially during political campaigns. A special type of lighting was developed for this purpose. It could range from torches on the ends of poles to specially made lanterns with painted glass panes, or even paper lanterns that closely resembled Oriental lighting fixtures (Plate 105). Specialized types of lighting for outdoor use were developed. Iron foundries that produced railings and balconies often turned their attention to making post lanterns that burned candles or gas (Plate 117).

Following the Philadelphia Centennial Exhibition of 1876, a strong interest developed in America's colonial past. Antiquarianism became popular, and reproductions of colonial furnishings began to be made—a trend that has lasted until the present. Candleholders were included in this group (Plate 122). Old lighting fixtures began to be collected for use in new colonial interiors. This trend is clearly shown in American paintings both sophisticated and primitive from the mid-century until its end (plates 123, 124, 125, 126, 127, 128, 129, 131, and 136). Especially in the still-life works of the *trompe l'œil* painters, such as Harnett, Peto, and Haberle, is this trend to be seen (plates 126, 127, 128, and 129).

By the 1890's historical revivalism had developed such confusion in design that a group of artists, architects, and designers who were principally European developed a style that completely contradicted revivalism—Art Nouveau. The style was based on the whiplash curve and organic forms. Curved lines and very little surface ornamentation are its chief characteristics. One of the few Americans who was involved in this development was Louis Comfort Tiffany (1848–1933), whose interpretation of the style won him international recognition.

Candleholders made of patinated bronze and glass were often among the most successful of his productions (Plate 133 and Plate 134). The metal part usually embraced some organic form that flowed in a single unit. Tiffany was a collector as well as a designer, and his famous New York City apartment revealed his interest in old or exotic lighting fixtures (Plate 135). Other American craftsmen were influenced by the English Arts and Crafts Movement and Art Nouveau, although their work seldom demonstrates the quality and understanding of Tiffany (Plate 132).

The Art Nouveau candleholders are the last treated here. The twentieth century has seen the development of myriad candleholder forms. However, these are generally not of interest to the collector, who is anxious to use candleholders that are harmonious with other period furnishings. Only time will give enough perspective to sort out the candleholders of this century. Now they are used for decorative and nostalgic purposes—a far cry from the necessity of early America.

136

101. Candelabrum (center of three-part set), brass (gilt finish), glass, and marble, Philadelphia, Cornelius and Co., c. 1840–1850. Historical revivalism is to be seen in all the elements of this centerpiece from a three-piece mantel set (two single candlesticks accompany it); Cornelius and Co. is the impressed mark. The subject is the American pioneer and the Indian. These sets were often called girandoles. By 1845 Cornelius and Co. were the largest producers of lamps and lighting fixtures in the United States. Height 18 inches.

The Metropolitan Museum of Art

102. Pair of candlesticks, brass (gilt finish), glass, and marble, American, c. 1840–1850. These candlesticks with coffin-cut prisms combine elements from the Gothic and Rococo revival styles. They are stamped "PATENT DEC. 18, 18(41?)" and depict the chapel at Mount Auburn Cemetery in Cambridge, Massachusetts, which was dedicated in 1831. Height 13⅝ inches. *Sleepy Hollow Restorations; gift of Mrs. Giles Whiting*

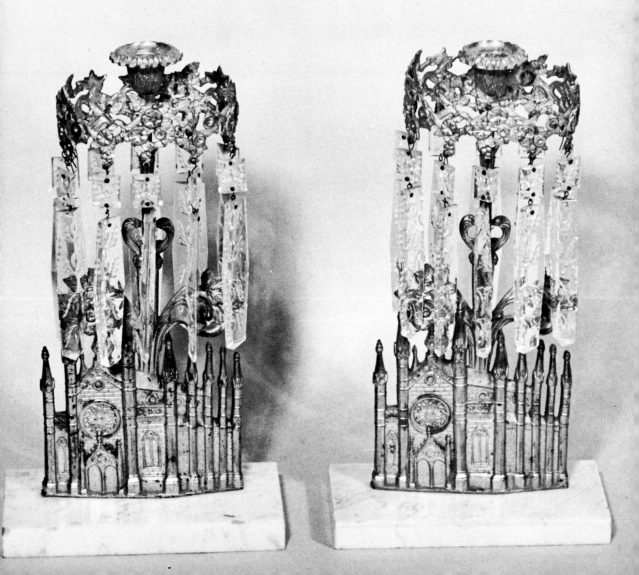

103. Candelabrum, brass (gilt finish), glass, and marble, American, c. 1840–1850. Here is another of the most popular patterns to be found in girandole sets—the bear and the beehive. The covering over the hive is Gothic and the foliage surrounding it is in the Rococo revival idiom. The coffin-shaped prisms and marble base are typical features. Height 16 inches.

Louis B. Young

104. Advertisement of Dietz, Brother & Co., New York City, c. 1840. The advertisement shows a number of lamps and candle fixtures the firm produced. At the bottom is a three-piece girandole set (see plates 100, 101, and 102), and at the top on either side are hall lanterns that probably burned candles. The remainder of the lighting fixtures shown are lamps.

Dietz & Company

105. Lantern, paper, American, c. 1848. Paper lanterns are extremely rare American lighting fixtures. This one has considerable historic significance because it is printed with the bust of George Washington over draped American flags and trophies. The flags depicted have thirty stars, which would indicate that Wisconsin had just joined the Union. Collapsible paper lanterns of this type are generally associated with political campaigns. Hence, the campaign of 1848 is suggested (Wisconsin being the newest state), when Zachary Taylor, a Whig, ran against Lewis Carr and Martin Van Buren. The presence of Washington's head would probably indicate that this was in support of Taylor, a fellow Whig. Height 12 inches (extended).

Sleepy Hollow Restorations

106. Pair of candlesticks, brass, possibly American, c. 1850. The Rococo revival is the principal design source embodied here. The bases, with their leafy standards and tortoises entwined with snakes, terminate in shafts that contain Rococo elements. The candle cups and *bobèche* are also Rococo. They belonged to Washington Irving, and were used by him at his home, Sunnyside, in Tarrytown, New York. Height 8¾ inches.

Sleepy Hollow Restorations

107. Pair of candlesticks, brass, American, c. 1853. These candlesticks of the eclectic revival type were used in the Robert Milligan house at Saratoga, New York, which was built in 1853. Two rooms from this house are presently installed at the Brooklyn Museum. Height 5¾ inches.

The Brooklyn Museum

108. Pair of candlesticks, brass and glass, American, c. 1853. The eccentric turning of the shafts and painted decoration of the bases and holders for prisms place these candlesticks in the eclectic revival idiom. They are from the Robert Milligan house at Saratoga, New York, which was built in 1853. Height 9⅜ inches.   *The Brooklyn Museum*

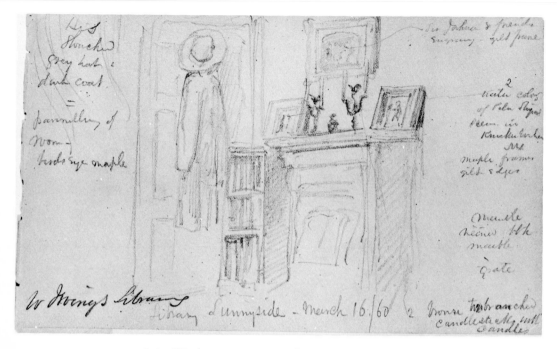

109. *Washington Irving's Library,* pencil on paper, Tarrytown, New York, Daniel Huntington (1816–1906), March 16, 1860. The drawing was done the year following Irving's death at Sunnyside. On the mantelpiece can be seen a pair of two-branched candelabra with birds as their center finial. Although these candelabra no longer exist at Sunnyside, it is interesting to notice their placement on the mantelpiece.

Cooper Union Museum for the Arts of Decoration

110. Candlestick, tinned sheet iron, American, 1853. The "hogscraper" is one of the most persistently used candlestick forms during the eighteenth and nineteenth centuries. The legend is that the base could be sharpened and used in butchering to scrape the bristles from a hog. These sticks invariably have an ejector for the stub of the candle, which would enable it to be used longer. Also, a hook is often present at the top, permitting the stick to be hung. Some examples have a brass trim around the neck and others an iron band. During the early nineteenth century vast numbers of hogscrapers marked "SHAW" were imported from Birmingham, England. The present example is stamped on the thumbpiece "PATENTED 1853." It is identical to a model in the Smithsonian Institution that was patented by Merriam, Harris, Wheeler, and Merriam on April 2, 1853. The patent is based on "Construction of Iron Candlestick." Height $5\frac{3}{16}$ inches.

Sleepy Hollow Restorations

145

111. Candlestick, tinned sheet iron painted, American, c. 1855. Next to the hogscraper, the chamberstick was probably the most universal form of the nineteenth century. The shaft, which was generally open as a long candle cup, rested on a deep saucer-shaped base, and could be carried by a ring handle; an ejector and douter are also provided. This example is one that Washington Irving had at Sunnyside at Tarrytown, New York. Height 5 inches. *Sleepy Hollow Restorations*

112. Candlestick, tinned sheet iron painted, American, c. 1855. This example is less elaborate than that shown in Plate 110, and from Plate 111 it is easy to see that this was a less-expensive type. It belonged to Washington Irving at Sunnyside in Tarrytown, New York. Height 2⅛ inches. *Sleepy Hollow Restorations*

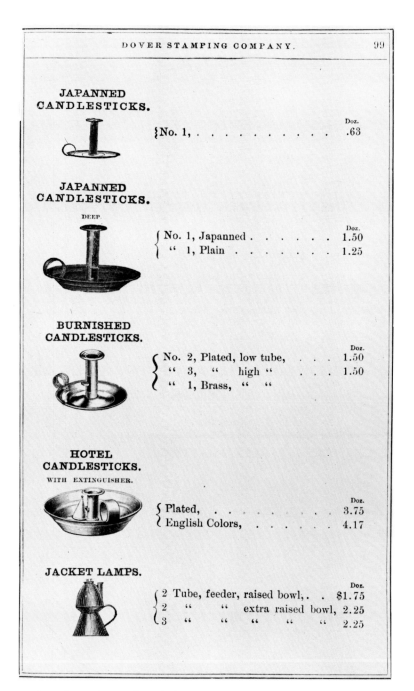

JAPANNED CANDLESTICKS.

Doz.

{No. 1, ...63

JAPANNED CANDLESTICKS.

DEEP.

Doz.

{ No. 1, Japanned 1.50
{ " 1, Plain 1.25

BURNISHED CANDLESTICKS.

Doz.

{ No. 2, Plated, low tube, . . . 1.50
{ " 3, " high " . . . 1.50
{ " 1, Brass, " "

HOTEL CANDLESTICKS.

WITH EXTINGUISHER.

Doz.

{ Plated, ... 3.75
{ English Colors, ... 4.17

JACKET LAMPS.

Doz.

{ 2 Tube, feeder, raised bowl, . . $1.75
{ 2 " " extra raised bowl, 2.25
{ 3 " " " " " 2.25

113. Page from the catalog of the Dover Stamping Company, Boston, 1895. That the tinned chambersticks were a persistent form during the nineteenth century is well illustrated here from a source of the end of the century. This shows quite well that the addition of ejectors and douters caused the price to rise. *Smithsonian Institution*

114. *Still Life with Candle, Open Book and Spectacles*, charcoal on paper, American, Anna C. Cobb, c. 1860. This charming drawing from the Civil War period depicts a chamberstick of the simplest type in use.

Museum of Fine Arts, Boston; M. and M. Karolik Collection

115. *Inspirational Drawing*, ink on paper, American, Sister Sally Lomise, May 20, 1847. Representations of candles and lamps are often seen in Shaker inspirational drawings. Here called "A heavenly Lamp" is a two-burner whale-oil lamp and a hogscraper candlestick (Plate 109).

Shaker Community, Inc.

116. Lantern, tinned sheet iron lacquered, and mica, American, John A. Minor, 1855. During the mid-nineteenth century many patents were secured for folding pocket lanterns. These were small cases in which a candle stub and matches could be carried; the case could then be converted into a lantern. They were often used for reading while traveling. The patent mark on the present example is "Minor's Patent, January 24, 1855." Height 3 inches.

Smithsonian Institution

No. 381 PATTERN.

Ornamental Wrought and Cast Iron Railing with Lamp Posts, 8 feet high, can be made higher if required, and without Lamp Posts.

117. Page from *Illustrated Catalogue of Iron Railings* . . . of J. W. Fiske, New York City, c. 1860. Lampposts topped with glass shades and metal fittings are provided in this iron fence. Such post lamps were very popular for use on either side of entrances to town houses. Sometimes they contained one candle socket, but often there were three or four.

Sleepy Hollow Restorations

118. Candelabrum, bronze, New York City, Mitchell Vance & Co., 1876. Eclecticism of design is reflected in this engraving of a candelabrum taken from Walter Smith's volume dealing with the Philadelphia Centennial Exhibition of 1876 (see Bibliography). While the supporting figure is generally classical, many other design elements are combined in the whole.

119. Candelabrum (one of a pair), bronze, American, c. 1875. Very similar to the example shown in Plate 118, the design elements here are not so confused as in the Philadelphia Centennial example. This and the following were owned by Senator Nelson W. Aldrich of Rhode Island and later by his daughter, Miss Lucy T. Aldrich. Height 22¾ inches.

Private Collection of the Rockefeller Family
of Pocantico Hills, New York

120. Candelabrum (one of a pair), bronze, American, c. 1875. This is the matching figure to Plate 119. Height 22¾ inches.

Private Collection of the Rockefeller Family
of Pocantico Hills, New York

154

121. Chandelier, brass, New York City, Mitchell Vance & Co., 1876. Another plate from Walter Smith's work on the Philadelphia Centennial Exhibition of 1876 (see Plate 118) clearly shows eclectic design in a massive chandelier intended for a church or public building. It is interesting that the surrounding arch is Moorish, but Near Eastern elements cannot be found in the chandelier.

122. Plate from Clarence Cook's *The House Beautiful,* which was published in 1878 (see Bibliography). Following the Centennial Exhibition of 1876, Americans began to take a greater interest in antiquarianism, and especially in colonial furnishings. The small candelabrum seen here is probably not an antique (that is, eighteenth-century), but rather a later nineteenth-century statement of what an early fixture was really like.

" How far that little candle throws his beams! "

123. *Ichabod Crane at a Ball at the Van Tassel Mansion,* oil on canvas, New York, John Quidor (1801–1881), 1855. In this canvas, Quidor is attempting to evoke the feeling of an early eighteenth-century Hudson River Valley interior. His treatment of the candlesticks is remarkable in a historical sense as they follow early forms (Plate 6 and Plate 7).

Sleepy Hollow Restorations

124. *Play Me a Tune,* oil on canvas, New York, Eastman Johnson (1824–1906), c. 1880. An early iron and brass candlestick is shown here in an effort to give an old-fashioned appearance to the room (Plate 25 and Plate 26). (Detail, top.) *Mrs. Giles Whiting; photograph courtesy Frick Art Reference Library*

125. *Country Dance*, oil on canvas, American, M. E. Ferrill, 1883. Primitive painters often vividly depict interiors. The two candlesticks shown here are certainly intended to be of the hogscraper variety, with brass bands on the shafts (Plate 109). Hanging inside the fireplace is a candle mold (Plate 2).   *Colonel and Mrs. Edgar W. Garbisch*

126. *Munich Still Life,* oil on canvas, American, William Michael Harnett (1848–1892), 1884. Harnett was one of the masters of *trompe l'œil* painting, and his still-life groups often contain candlesticks. The one shown here is of the Federal baluster-turned type (Plate 72).   *Newark Museum*

159

127. *Still Life,* oil on canvas, American, William Michael Harnett (1848–1892), c. 1890. A saucer-base candlestick is to be seen in this vivid painting (plates 110, 111, and 112).   *Miss Helen C. Frick; photograph courtesy Frick Art Reference Library*

128. *After Night's Study*, oil on canvas, American, John Frederick Peto
(1854–1907), c. 1885. There is a false Harnett signature on this canvas
that is misleading. The hogscraper candlestick is shown in great detail
(Plate 109). *The Detroit Institute of Arts*

129. *Grandma's Hearthstone*, oil on canvas, American, John Haberle (1856–1933), 1890. Another of the *trompe l'œil* painters, Haberle shows several lighting fixtures in this delightful scene. There are two hogscrapers with brass bands (Plate 109) and a punched lantern of the "Paul Revere" type (Plate 94). Also on the mantelpiece is a tray with a pair of snuffers (Plate 53).   *The Detroit Institute of Arts*

130. Plate from Putnam's *The Open Fireplace in All Ages,* which was published in 1886 (see Bibliography). Although gas was the principal illuminant by this time, that candles were still in use can be gathered from this engraving of a fashionable Boston parlor. Sconces are used on either side of the looking glass for decoration as well as for practical purposes.

131. *By the Fireside,* oil on canvas, American, unknown artist, c. 1890. Total antiquarianism is to be seen in this delightful primitive. It depicts a scene from Denman Thompson's play *The Old Homestead,* which opened in Boston in April, 1886. A single candlestick stands on the mantelshelf.

Abby Aldrich Rockefeller Folk Art Collection

132. Candlestick, bronze, American, Charles H. Barr, 1899. This plate comes from *The House Beautiful* for December, 1899, in an article on "Metal-work and Amateurs." In this candlestick, flowing lines and asymmetry of Art Nouveau design are well demonstrated. The saucer-based stick is provided with a holder for matches and a conical douter for extinguishing the flame.

133. Two candlesticks, bronze and glass, New York City, Louis Comfort Tiffany (1848–1933), c. 1900. Tiffany was America's greatest exponent of Art Nouveau. His understanding of this movement is often best shown in his lamps and candlesticks. The stick to the left has an organic root base, and the one to the right is composed around a group of iridescent glass balls. Both are stamped "TIFFANY STUDIOS NEW YORK." Height (left) 9 inches, (right) 9½ inches.   *The Museum of Modern Art;*
The Joseph H. Heil Tiffany Collection

134. Three candlesticks, bronze and glass, New York City, Louis Comfort Tiffany, c. 1900. At the center is a more elaborate root-base candlestick with swirled opaque glass candle cup and shade. The pair terminate in heavy ball feet. All are stamped "TIFFANY STUDIOS NEW YORK." Height (left and right) 9 inches, (center) 18½ inches.   *Author's Collection*

135. Plate from Desmond and Croly's *Stately Homes in America*, which was published in 1903 (see Bibliography). The New York City apartment of Louis Comfort Tiffany was considered one of the great wonders of the city. A variety of lighting fixtures and ornaments is seen hanging from the ceiling. Some of the lights appear to be Near Eastern, and burned oil and candles.

136. *A New England Woman*, oil on canvas, American, Cecilia Beaux (1853–1942), c. 1900. That antiquarianism was still popular at the end of the nineteenth century is well shown here. The old woman sits in a country Chippendale chair, and the candlestand beside her contains a saucer-base chamberstick in which the candle has been extinguished by a douter (plates 110, 111, and 112).   *Pennsylvania Academy of the Fine Arts*

Bibliography

Books

d'Allemagne, Henri-René. *Histoire du Luminaire*. Paris, 1891.

Barret, Richard Carter. *Bennington Pottery and Porcelain*. New York, 1958.

Biddle, James. *American Art from American Collectors*. Loan exhibition: Metropolitan Museum of Art, New York, 1963.

Bigelow, Francis Hill. *Historic Silver of the Colonies and Its Makers*. New York, 1917.

Buhler, Kathryn C. *American Silver*. Cleveland, 1950.

———. *Mount Vernon Silver*. Mount Vernon, Va., 1957.

Butler, Joseph T. *American Antiques 1800–1900*. New York, 1965.

Cook, Clarence. *The House Beautiful*. New York, 1878.

Curle, Alexander O. *Fourteenth to Eighteenth Century Candlesticks*. Unpublished manuscript, London, n.d.

Davidson, Marshall B. *Life in America*. 2 vols., New York, 1951.

Desmond, Harry W., and Herbert Croly. *Stately Homes in America*. New York, 1903.

Dietz, Fred. *A Leaf from the Past, Dietz Then and Now*. New York, 1914.

Dillaby, Mrs. Frank H. (Ed.). *The Twenty-fifth Anniversary of the Rushlight Club*. Newton, Mass., 1957.

Dover Stamping Company Catalogue. Boston, 1895.

Earle, Alice Morse. *Homelife in Colonial Days*. New York, 1898.

Ensko, Stephen G. C. *American Silversmiths and Their Marks III*. New York, 1948.

Fales, Martha Gandy. *American Silver in the Henry Francis du Pont Winterthur Museum*. Winterthur, Del., 1958.

Ford, Alice. *Pictorial Folk Art, New England to California*. New York and London, 1949.

Frankenstein, Alfred. *After the Hunt: William Harnett and Other American Still-Life Painters, 1870–1900*. Berkeley and Los Angeles, 1953.

Gallery of Fine Arts, Yale University. *Masterpieces of New England Silver 1650–1800*. Loan exhibition. New Haven, 1939.

Gould, Mary Earle. *Antique Tin and Tole Ware*. Rutland, Vt., 1958.

Hayward, Arthur H. *Colonial Lighting*. New York, 1962.

Hough, Walter. *Collection of Heating and Lighting Utensils in the United States National Museum*. Washington, D.C., 1928.

Illustrated Catalogue of Iron Railings. J. W. Fiske and Co., New York, n.d.

Kauffman, Henry J. *Early American Copper, Tin, and Brass*. New York, 1950.

Kerfoot, J. B. *American Pewter*. New York, 1924.

Lee, Ruth Webb. *Early American Pressed Glass*. Northborough, Mass., 1931.

———. *Sandwich Glass*. Northborough, Mass., 1944.

———. *Victorian Glass*. Northborough, Mass., 1944.

Lindsay, J. Seymour. *Iron and Brass Implements of the English and American Home*. Boston and London, n.d.

McKearin, George S. and Helen. *American Glass*. New York, 1941.

Mercer, Henry C. *Light and Fire Making*. Doylestown, Pa., 1898.

The Metropolitan Museum of Art. *Early American Silver*. Picture Book. New York, 1955.

Museum of Fine Arts, Boston. *Colonial Silversmiths, Masters and Apprentices*. Loan exhibition. Boston, 1956.

————. *M. and M. Karolik Collection of American Paintings, 1815–1865*. Cambridge, Mass., 1949.

Newark Museum. *Classical America, 1815–1845*. Loan exhibition. Newark, N. J., 1963.

Nutting, Wallace. *Furniture Treasury*. 3 vols. New York, 1948.

Pearce, Mrs. John N. *The White House*. Washington, D.C., 1962.

Percier, Charles and Pierre-François L. Fontaine. *Recueil de Décorations Intérieures . . .* Paris, 1812.

Phillips, John Marshall. *American Silver*. New York, 1949.

Putnam, J. Pickering. *The Open Fireplace in All Ages*. Boston, 1886.

Ramsay, John. *American Potters and Pottery*. Clinton, Mass., 1939.

Richardson, E. P. *Painting in America*. New York, 1956.

Robins, F. W. *The Story of the Lamp (and the Candle)*. London, 1939.

Roy, L. M. A. *The Candle Book*. Brattleboro, Vt., 1938.

Smith, Walter. *The Masterpieces of the Centennial International Exhibition*. Vol. II, *Industrial Art*. Philadelphia, 1876.

Sonn, Albert H. *Early American Wrought Iron*. 3 vols. New York, 1928.

Thwing, Leroy. *Flickering Flames*. Rutland, Vt., 1958.

————. (Trans. and Ed.). *Old Lamps of Central Europe and Other Lighting Devices*. Rutland, Vt., 1963.

The Virginia Museum of Fine Arts. *Masterpieces of American Silver*. Loan exhibition. Richmond, 1960.

Watkins, C. Malcolm. *Artificial Lighting in America, 1830–1860*. Washington, D.C., 1952.

Wechssler-Kümmel, Sigrid. *Schöne Lampen Leuchter und Laternen*. Heidelberg and Munich, 1962.

Wildenstein Galleries. *Three Hundred Years of New York City Families*. Loan exhibition. New York, 1966.

Periodicals

Baagøe, Johan Hedemann. "Style Patterns in Candlesticks," *The Rushlight*, February, 1966, pp. 7–15.

Barber, William P., Jr. "An Unusual Tin Mirror Candle Sconce," *The Rushlight*, August, 1955, pp. 17–18.

Coons, Quentin L. "Pewter Candlesticks," *The Rushlight*, April, 1939, pp. 3–4.

————. "Pocket Lanterns," *The Rushlight*, June, 1946, pp. 4–12.

Coons, Mrs. Quentin L. "Snuffers and Candle Accessories," *The Rushlight*, May, 1948, pp. 1–10.

Gaines, Edith. "Quillwork: American Paper Filigree," *Antiques*, December, 1960, pp. 562–565.

Godden, Geoffrey A. "Fairy Lamps for Collectors," *The Rushlight*, May, 1966. pp. 15–17.

Grimwade, A. G. "Silver at Althorp, II: The Candlesticks and Candelabra," *The Connoisseur*, March, 1963, pp. 159–165.

Hayward, Arthur H. "Iron in Early American Lighting," *Antiques*, May, 1923, pp. 222–224.

Hayward, J. F. "Candlesticks with Figure Stems," *The Connoisseur*, January, 1963, pp. 16–21.

Hebard, Helen B. "Candles," *The Rushlight*, June, 1947, pp. 1–11.

Hughes, G. Bernard. "A Chronology of English Candlesticks," *Antiques*, March, 1930, pp. 234–237.

———. "Old English Candle Snuffers," *Antiques*, November, 1946, pp. 316–318.

———. "Silver Candlesticks and Candelabra," *Country Life Annual*, 1956, pp. 97–100.

Huntley, Richmond. "Candlesticks of Various Sorts," *American Collector*, May, 1942, p. 12.

Kjellberg, Pierre. "Le Lustre de Cristal sous Toutes ses Formes Classiques," *Connaissance des Arts*, July, 1963, pp. 60–67.

Little, Nina Fletcher. "References to Lighting in Colonial Records," *The Rushlight*, March, 1941, pp. 5–10.

"Metal-work and Amateurs," *The House Beautiful*, December, 1899, pp. 16–24.

Oman, Charles. "English Brass Chandeliers in American Churches," *Antiques*, August, 1966, pp. 192–194.

Ormsbee, Thomas H. "Candlesticks from Sandwich and Points West," *American Collector*, December, 1937, pp. 10–11.

Penzer, N. M. "The Plate at Knole—II." *The Connoisseur*, May, 1961, pp. 178–184.

Raymond, Percy E. "Candles," *The Rushlight*, September, 1945, pp. 3–5.

———. "Lanterns," *The Rushlight*, March, 1946, pp. 3–7.

Roe, F. Gordon. "Old Brass Candlesticks," *Antiques*, June, 1938, pp. 314–318.

Rollins, Edwin B. "Candles and Candle Customs," *The Rushlight*, March, 1941, pp. 2–3.

Rushford, Edward A. "Pierced Lanterns Date from 1500," *American Collector*, May, 1937, p. 1.

Schlumberger, Eveline. "Caffiéri," *Connaissance des Arts*, May, 1965, pp. 76–87.

Sherlock, Robert. "The Cheltenham Chandelier," *The Connoisseur*, February, 1965, pp. 81–85.

Susswein, Rita. "Early 19th Century New York Produced Fine Glass," *American Collector*, January 23, 1934, p. 3.

Thomas, W. G. Mackay. "Brass Candlesticks in Queen Anne's Reign," *Country Life*, September 13, 1946, pp. 484–485.

Thwing, Leroy L. "Candles," *Antiques*, December, 1940, pp. 273–275.

———. "Torches, Tapers and Candles," *The Rushlight*, August, 1950, pp. 3–12.

———. "Torches, Tapers and Candles" (Part II), *The Rushlight*, November, 1950, pp. 3–9.

Twose, G. M. R. "Form and Function in Relation to Candlesticks," *The House Beautiful*, January, 1900, pp. 95–96.

Van Rensselaer, Stephen. "American Tin Candle Sconces," *Antiques*, August, 1936, pp. 58–59.

Waugh, Naomi. "Burglar's Horror," *American Collector*, September, 1940, pp. 10–11.

Wenham, Edward. "Candlesticks in Silver," *The Antique Collector*, June, 1956, pp. 93–98.

———. "Candlesticks and Snuffers by American Silversmiths," *Antiques*, December, 1930, pp. 491–493.

Index